POLICE
NONLETHAL
FORCE
MANUAL

POLICE NONLETHAL FORCE MANUAL

Your Choices
This Side of Deadly

Bill Clede

*In collaboration with Dr. Kevin Parsons,
Justice System Training Association*

*Photos by Bill Clede
unless otherwise credited*

Stackpole Books

Published by
STACKPOLE BOOKS
Cameron and Kelker Streets
P.O. Box 1831
Harrisburg, PA 17105

Printed in the United States of America

10   9   8   7   6   5   4   3   2

Library of Congress Cataloging-in-Publication Data

Clede, Bill.
   Police nonlethal force manual.

   1. Police training — United States.   2. Police
psychology.   I. Parsons, Kevin.   II. Title.
HV8142.C44   1987   363.2′32   87-6458
ISBN 0-8117-1300-8

Contents

Acknowledgments

Add up the years of experience of the experts who provided the knowledge, skills, techniques, and principles described herein and it would total several lifetimes. They are cited throughout the text and are identified in the appendix. These experts are all concerned with police training. They are not necessarily affiliated with and do not necessarily endorse JSTA or any other association. They are dedicated educators who so strongly desire that officers we send into harm's way are the best prepared we can make them, that they were eager to share their expertise with me. They are all active trainers and appreciate that giving you an understanding of what they are teaching will make the efforts of all defensive-tactics instructors more productive and your learning quicker and easier. What they have to tell you will give you many more choices to apply before a situation degenerates to the point of requiring deadly force.

Publisher's Note

This book presents an understanding of some of the options you might use to fulfill your responsibilities as a police officer. You must be personally trained in the proper application of these techniques by a qualified instructor. This book is not intended to be a substitute for such training. Misapplication or misuse of any technique or tool, whether discussed here or not, may make you vulnerable to a lawsuit. The publisher, consultants, and author accept no liability of any sort for any personal injury or property damage that might result from the use or misuse of any of the techniques or applications presented or implied in this book.

Foreword

I first met Bill Clede when he assumed the position as public relations counsel to Smith & Wesson ten years ago. During that period, Bill developed a close working relationship with police trainers throughout the United States. His willingness to follow up on problems, ability to find answers to complex questions, and continual assistance to training bureaus earned him a large number of close friends in the law enforcement community.

Bill Clede's two previous works, *Police Handgun Manual* and *Police Shotgun Manual,* have received wide distribution and acclaim in the law enforcement field. It was with this foundation that he tackled the project of a book on less lethal alternatives for law enforcement personnel. When he contacted me for assistance, I was pleased to lend my support. As Executive Director of the Justice System Training Association, I welcomed the opportunity to assist him in providing insight into an area all too often overlooked by agencies. Here was an opportunity for trainers from throughout the nation to acquaint fellow officers with techniques and procedures developed through long hours of research in their specific fields of specialization.

In the chapters that follow you will be exposed to some of the most respected police instructors in the nation. Bill's monumental task has been to bring together in one format some of the most sophisticated training currently available in this country. In his own straightforward, street-oriented style, this text is an effort to acquaint the readers with what is available on the forefront of defensive measures training.

All of us who have been involved in the development of this book, as well as the law enforcement community in general, owe Bill Clede our gratitude for taking the time to meet with us, go through our training and introduce the law enforcement community to the techniques that we believe to be so important for the safe performance of the policing function.

Read the text carefully, study the concepts in detail. Here in one publication you will receive an overview of tactics and techniques that are designed to facilitate your survival and enhance the professionalism with which you serve your community.

Kevin Parsons, Ph.D.
Appleton, Wisconsin

Prologue

The policeman is armed and everyone knows it. But there are strict limitations on when you can use that gun you carry. And the scumbags know that, too.

Jerry Lane, director of OffShoots Training Institute, tells a story of when he was on the Dallas Police Department. He and his partner responded to a domestic disturbance and found the disheveled couple in heated confrontation. The woman was hysterical. The man was stark naked, irrationally flailing a big butcher knife around. He jumped up onto the coffee table and warned the officers to stay away.

Now, Jerry's a level-headed and soft-spoken lad. The man wasn't threatening to attack him. He knew Jerry couldn't shoot. Jerry told the man politely to put the knife down and, much to his surprise, the man glanced at Jerry's partner, slowly laid the knife on the table, and presented his wrists for cuffing.

Astonished, Jerry asked the man what made him change his mind.

"I knew you couldn't shoot as long as I didn't threaten you with the knife," the man said. "But when I seen your partner behind you with his fingers stopping up his ears, I figured he knew somethin' I didn't know."

Many bad guys are as experienced with the law as you are. They know what they can get away with and they'll get away with everything they can — unless the consequences might affect their own well-being. The armed robber, fleeing a scene, will sweep his escape route clean, and it doesn't matter to him if you are standing in his way. He won't feel compassion for your wife and kids.

His need is to get away and he'll eliminate any obstacle to his escape. Any consequences you suffer are *your problem.*

The exception to this extreme example is if the obstacle will likely impose greater consequences on *him.*

Of course there are exceptions but, as a rule, if the criminal *believes* you will shoot, he'll stop and raise his hands. He isn't dumb enough to get himself killed. Regardless of the law or department policies, a perpetrator's perception of what you *might* do is a greater influence on him than what you are *permitted* to do. Unfortunately, for you, the U.S. Supreme Court and the media have educated the criminal element that your justifications for shooting are much more limited today than they used to be.

This principle applies throughout your dealings with the public. The schoolboy crosses at your crosswalk because, if he doesn't, you might tell his mother. The motorist who sneaks through a red light is most apologetic because he might get a warning rather than a ticket. The scruffy brawler in a barroom backs off when you draw your baton because it can hurt him more than your fists.

But how do too many police recruits go through training? One state's curriculum provides six hours of "defensive tactics" and 40 hours of "firearms." That's nearly seven times as much time spent on deadly force as on nonlethal control measures.

Andrew Casavant of the Midwest Tactical Training Institute polled his classes about their ongoing in-service training. How many receive unarmed defensive training? Usually none. How many are trained with their impact weapon? Perhaps two out of 40. How many have ever had to use their guns? Usually none.

But ask how many have had to physically subdue a subject or handcuff a struggling suspect, and almost all hands will go up.

It stands to reason that you will be called upon to exercise control over a subject in nonlethal situations many times more than you will ever have to resort to the ultimate measure of control—deadly force.

Yet the emphasis in training is on firearms. Even firearms instructors are concerned, "If we stress the gun in threat response, are we predisposing our officers to *always* respond with the gun?"

When you pull your gun and fire, it means that all other control techniques were inappropriate, or were tried and failed. It means that the only way you could stop the aggressor's felonious assault was to shoot before he caused death or grievous bodily harm.

Remember, that's the *only* reason you shoot—TO STOP THE AGGRESSOR'S FELONIOUS ASSAULT BEFORE HE CAUSES DEATH OR GRIEVOUS BODILY HARM.

You know very well that most situations are faced before the point of deadly force is reached. Most will never require gunplay. But all too many, these days, require definite and decisive control measures to resolve them before ultimate force is needed.

Yet the emphasis in training has been on the gun. Too little time has been spent on gaining compliance with techniques short of deadly force. Happily, I think this trend is changing. Firearms instructors themselves promote the idea that the gun is simply the end of the force continuum. It is the *final* alternative — and it must be justifiable, or you're in trouble.

If you are trained only with your sidearm, you have only a few options to use in resolving a confrontation. If you are trained in defensive tactics, you have many options, many possible alternatives. That is the value of learning and practicing as many nonlethal force techniques as you can. You may be able to resolve a confrontation with a simple grip on the guy's arm that causes him pain, before he pushes you into a knock-down-drag-out situation.

But there's a catch. No book, by itself, will make you an expert. You didn't learn mathematics by reading about numbers. You had to work sample problems. You didn't learn to swim or drive a car from a book. You couldn't really learn to shoot well all by yourself. Learning any physical skill requires hands-on practice under the watchful eye of a qualified instructor, especially so with defensive tactics. You have to feel it, practice it, become so familiar with it that your actions come naturally, without having to think about them. Your actions become reflexive.

There is more to defensive techniques than what we can cover here. This book aims to give you an understanding of the techniques discussed, and to explain how and why they work. Armed with this knowledge, you will get much more out of training sessions you are lucky enough to attend. You will more quickly become competent in controlling a subject, and defending yourself against an aggressor.

Some 17 percent of the nation's police officers are assaulted each year, 83 percent of them with *human* weapons (such as hands, fists and feet), according to the Uniform Crime Reports. It's obviously in your own best interest to take as much advantage as you can of whatever training you can get in nonlethal force.

Bill Clede

1

Fitness Is for Everybody

America is on a fitness kick, but you know that. But do you really understand what fitness is? And do you realize how important it is for the police officer?

It shocked me to learn that research conducted at the University of Southern California Stress Laboratory by Dr. William Crowe found the average police officer lives to be 59; only one in 10 lives past 60.

Regardless of the physical demands of the job, if you want to enjoy your golden years, you'd be well advised to embark on a regular fitness program that accomplishes the multiple goals of extending your longevity, as well as making you a more effective police officer.

But before we presume our need for fitness, consider the controversy that has been stirred when requirements are imposed on the older desk men.

Required skills must be job related. Instructors develop their training programs on the basis of job relatedness. But courts considering such cases have asked, "Just what do officers do?" One study showed officers spent most of their time sitting in squad cars. The court might conclude that the job-related physical activity is lifting a coffee cup.

Courts have rejected the argument that an officer should be physically fit because he might have to run or struggle with a suspect someday. But courts have ruled in favor of an overall health and well-being approach.

Dr. Kenneth Cooper, of the Aerobics Institute in Dallas, Texas, cites "balance" as the key to equilibrium. He identifies three factors for healthful well-being: (1) aerobic exercise, (2) a positive eating plan, and (3) emotional equilibrium. And he agrees with the one police fitness specialist I found during my research for this book.

Aerobic means using oxygen. Aerobic exercises include physical activities that increase the heart rate: swimming, bicycling, running, jumping rope, walking, cross-country skiing. Medical research shows there is a correlation between aerobic exercise and a more efficient heart and lung capacity.

Emotional equilibrium refers to dealing with stress in a positive way. Research has shown that psychological stress leads to psychological problems.

1.1 A Police Fitness Expert

A former police chief in a small upstate Wisconsin town, Tim Powers, made a study of police fitness. He became so concerned that the unique demands of police fitness weren't being met that he quit his job and started the Fitness Institute for Police, Fire and Rescue in Menasha, Wisconsin. Now he is a police performance specialist. He analyzes performance needs of a department, then designs a fitness program to provide a sound physical foundation on which officers can build to accomplish their goals.

We talked for nearly an hour and finally I asked, "Tim, we've discussed a lot of things, but just how much time would a policeman have to invest to maintain a high-performance conditioning level?"

"Once we've identified just what it is a particular situation needs, a fitness program could require as little as one hour, three days a week."

That's a pretty cheap price to pay for a longer life, improved performance, and better survivability in confrontations.

1.2 Two Types of Fitness

Health fitness is one thing. Everybody needs to be healthy. Health is basic to life.

Physical fitness is another. Sure, there are the health club routines designed for the general public. But the demands on the general public aren't the same as the demands on police officers. A fitness program for police needs to be designed to meet the demands of the law enforcement profession.

Law enforcement has a high stress level—higher than most jobs. A policeman is expected to change in 0 to 3 seconds from a state of total rest sitting in a cruiser, to a state of total intensity on a high-risk call.

1.3 Stress Management

But a policeman often doesn't recognize when he is under stress. He may begin to see himself snapping at the kids, drinking more than he should, having few social contacts outside of his fraternity, becoming dissatisfied with the job without knowing why. These are all signs of stress that should tip you off to the idea that you need to do something to cope with yourself before you, too, wind up in divorce court.

1.4 Three Major Areas of Concern

A police fitness program must address three major concerns: mental conditioning, nutrition, and exercise.

Mentally, you can consciously think yourself into relaxing in stress situations. Keeping calm helps you cope, lets you think more clearly, improves your chances for survival. Fast, shallow breaths are associated with stress. You can mentally tell yourself to breathe slowly, deeply.

Nutrition is simply a matter of eating a balanced diet, eating the right things at the right time, and eating sensibly. My downfall is coffee and doughnuts — bad for nutrition.

1.5 Four Exercise Targets

A comprehensive police exercise program should address four categories of concern.

1.5.1 Cardiovascular-Respiration

Sudden cardiac arrest is the biggest killer of police officers. A properly designed program improves the heart function, improves blood circulation, and increases your lung capacity. By training through aerobic conditioning, you'll find yourself better able to exert the explosive power you sometimes need to handle a situation.

1.5.2 Muscle Strength and Stamina

Your punch power isn't increased by doing biceps curls. It's exercised by punching, by doing the function you want to improve. A qualified law enforcement physical training instructor can devise many simple routines that address the strengths a policeman needs.

1.5.3 Joint Flexibility

If you have freedom of movement, you can better perform the defensive tactics techniques that can save your skin. If your joints are stiff, your performance will suffer.

1.5.4 Reduce and Maintain Low Body Fat

It's a fact that excess body fat impairs coordinated body movement. The fat literally gets in the way. Do you get red in the face when you bend over to tie your shoes?

1.6 Fitness Is Worth It

You don't need the equipment of a health club gym to conduct an effective police exercise program; rather, you need a combination of such tools, according to Powers.

"More important are the principles of achieving your desired result," Powers explains. "Two milk cartons filled with sand can do the same thing as a $5,000 machine, if you use them right."

Perhaps this hits as close to home for you as it does for me. My wife and my doctor keep telling me to lose weight. Well, 195 isn't bad for a 5'11" guy. Okay, so 185 would be better and 175 would be better yet. So what! What would it mean to me if I lost 10 or 20 pounds?

How about a longer life? Is that worth three hours a week? How about improved job performance? A promotion would mean more money, now and later. And what about improving my chances of surviving a confrontation?

You can talk all you want about the "joy" of feeling better; reaching retirement age at a higher pay scale, then living to enjoy it, should be all the reason you need to be concerned about fitness.

"Since it's so easy to do, departments should build in an exercise program on duty," Powers says. "Productivity and morale go up. Absenteeism and sickness go down. The taxpayers get a better employee.

"And crime is bound to go down when the officers are doing a better job."

2

Psychology of Confrontation

There was a popular country song that talked about being a lover, not a fighter. And I think that's true for most people, including policemen. No one wants to hurt anybody. Policemen become hardened to street values over time, but it's not human nature.

Yet, the policeman is told he has the authority and responsibility to do whatever is necessary to protect and to serve our citizenry.

During wartime, a soldier's mind is conditioned to hate the enemy. He's the one who sacked the Alamo, sank the Maine, torpedoed the Lusitania, blitzed Poland, bombed Pearl Harbor, crossed the 49th Parallel, and invaded those nice people in South Viet Nam. He set up concentration camps and death camps to slaughter the Jews, raped the women, killed the children, tortured prisoners, and committed all kinds of atrocities for which he deserves to DIE.

But the soldier is either at home in a rear echelon or he's in the battlefield. He can't be in both at the same time. But for the policeman, the rear echelon IS the battlefield.

You might pull over the little old lady who ran a red light and a few minutes later face a terrorist group robbing a bank with automatic weapons. The policeman is one minute a father figure and the next an "exterminator."

What does that do to a cop's head?

Andrew Casavant of the Midwest Tactical Training Institute has pondered this question, queried qualified psychiatrists and psychologists, and shared with me his consensus.

Mental perspectives are critical to your surviving any confrontation. And these mental attitudes must be habitual, instinctive. All the physical skills in the world will be fruitless if your head is in the wrong place at the wrong time. Physical skills alone do not insure success.

There are a host of elements that insure your success in a confrontation, beyond the simple attributes of ability, power, speed, strength, balance, and reaction time.

These elements are to be found *in your mind.*

Merely knowing, remembering, or attempting defensive control techniques will neither defuse an assault nor guarantee your personal protection.

Mental conditioning is as necessary as the physical involvement.

According to Casavant, violent confrontations require the participants to be involved both physically and mentally. You must react with both mind and body if you are to be effective. Without the mental involvement, the physical technique is less effective, or totally useless. If you aren't mentally prepared, you are as useless as the little old lady who knows nothing will ever happen to her.

Mental preparedness, mental conditioning, the mental trigger — it has been called many things. But what does it mean?

The mentality that one needs to survive must begin at an early time and continue throughout training until the thoughts and subsequent actions become habitual — even in combat.

How do you develop this mentality and maintain it? Of what importance is it in a confrontational situation?

Casavant's theory is that before you can become physically skillful in defensive control techniques, there must be a transition from "what was" to "what is."

"What was" is how one views his past experience and perspectives on use of force in dealing with physical assaults. Before you became a cop, your life experiences were hardly aggressive. Now, those experiences interfere with your new role as a law enforcer.

"What is" reflects the environment in which you now operate. The Marquis of Queensbury rules don't matter any more. There's no referee to count to ten. No umpire to confirm that was a strike. There isn't even a union arbitrator to negotiate your grievances.

Once you accept the fact that no one is there to call the shots, to help out, you are well on the way to understanding what mental awareness is, and how it can enhance your physical skills. Even if help is by your side, they likely won't or can't do what needs to be done. You've got to take care of Number One: yourself.

What mentality is needed to insure your survival? Casavant has organized these attitudes in terms of what you face on the street.

2.1 Alertness

Alertness is the overriding theme. If you're not ready when it's time to act, your skills won't help. Presume that you can and probably will be assaulted. You immediately assess the threat. That's part of awareness, an awareness of where you are in relation to all things in your environment.

It's a fact that most people are unaware of their surroundings. Why should you be any different? Yes, training and experience prepares you. That can give you an edge. But only if you recognize what you are up against.

Jeff Cooper, a well-known combat shooting instructor in Arizona, came up with a color code scheme that police trainers have adopted with fervor.

2.1.1 Color Codes

1. WHITE: When you are home watching television, sleep-walking, totally unaware of your surroundings. Unfortunately, this is where most of the population spends its time. This is having the "victim" mentality, Casavant says; the "I can't believe it's happening to me" syndrome.
2. YELLOW: Now you are aware of your surroundings. You are relaxed but alert. You anticipate, rather than expect, something to happen. You are simply prepared.
3. ORANGE: Now you are aware of something specific in your surroundings that has caught your attention. Perhaps it will be a threat. You analyze the threat potential and potential risks to you and others.
4. RED: You are ready to do what needs to be done. You may decide to move in or back off, depending on the circumstance. But do you have a plan? If you don't, you'll probably lose, unless Lady Luck is sitting in your corner. If you do, your reaction will be quick and sure.
5. BLACK: You've got no choice. An assault is in progress. If you aren't mentally prepared, you PANIC. You must go from White (totally unaware) to Black (he shoots) in a fraction of a second. If you haven't followed the crucial self-training of always anticipating an attack, you add to the sad statistics. With anticipation comes preparedness.

It is critical to your survival that your own attitude is to be prepared when your wildest anticipation comes true.

2.2 Decisiveness

Once you commit to a reaction to a threat, be decisive about it, Casavant says. Hesitation, when the situation calls for action, can be fatal. A mind cluttered with liability issues, department policies, and other such diversions, will cause hesitation when you need to ACT. Make up your mind about those "what if" things beforehand, so that your decision is already made when the situation arises. When you are called upon to act, you can.

When the compliant "yes" person turns into a "maybe," then resists, he's a "no" person. You have to do something. Whatever you decide to do, DO IT.

2.3 Aggressiveness

You've decided to do it, so do it like you mean it. Be aggressive. You decide on a course of action—to apply a pain compliance technique, to use enough force to make it work. If you draw your baton, USE IT, hard—and properly. Don't pussyfoot around. End the confrontation with whatever force is necessary, as quickly as you can. This minimizes the risks to all involved.

But "aggressiveness" must be taught. It's not *our* human nature. And certainly not the nature of smaller statured male or petite female officers. You must learn to be assertive. That's part of defensive tactics training.

2.4 Speed

To execute any defensive tactics technique, to gain the advantage of surprise, you must act quickly. Speed is essential. First, speed of thought. Don't stop to ask yourself if he really meant to swing that lead pipe at you. Quick thinking is as important as quick hands or feet. Without speed of thought, actions are simply movements with no direction.

2.5 Calmness

Remaining cool and calm in any confrontation, both mentally and physically, is paramount to success. Through realistic training, you must learn to control your emotions through such sound physiological principles as adrenalin flow and respiration.

When you are involved in defending yourself or others, the seriousness of the situation is under your control. If you can decide a confrontation quickly and without injury, you minimize the seriousness of the attack.

Controlling yourself lets you control the situation before it gets out of hand—or controls you.

2.6 Ruthlessness

While it seems harsh, ruthlessness has a place in describing the mentality of a conflict. Ruthless means that we will win, and we will do whatever it takes to win, and survive. We will continue to fight, even if hurt, and we will never give up. When the situation calls for it, we will get "junkyard dog mean."

Ruthlessness is a state of mind that must be short-lived. If you can't let go after the need for force is past, you're being brutal. Being ruthless, when you must be ruthless, gives you the spirit for combat.

2.7 Surprise

If you strike when least expected, take your assailant down without warning, you gain the element of surprise. And that makes your technique even more effective.

2.8 A Perspective on Defense

The psychology of personal protection is neither sensational nor lackadaisical. It is as intense and as serious as your motivation for professionalism. It does not lie in peer attitudes or department requirements (if any). The responsibility is yours. Only you will determine your ability to respond to a threat. If you achieve the tactical transition of mind and body, of skill and psyche, you will succeed. You will survive.

Your desire to learn will determine your capacity for learning. If the class you attend is a "requirement," you won't get much out of it. If you recognize that the class may help you get home to your wife after work, you'll benefit. Do you want to win and survive? Training is a small price to pay to develop the skills and habits that enable you to win and survive.

The old adage that you will do under stress what you've trained to do is really not quite correct. You will probably perform much worse in a serious confrontation than you ever did in training. So, to survive a street confrontation, you need to continually exercise the skills you learned in class. And you can do it in your head.

2.9 Mental Exercises

Suppose that little old lady were to swing her umbrella at your head. What would you do? Imagine yourself doing what you need to do to parry her blow. Suppose someone leaped out from the dark corner with a gun in his hand. What would you do? Draw and shoot? Or dive for cover? And where's cover?

If you can actually see yourself going through the motions of your newly learned techniques, it will improve your ability to respond quickly. While there's no substitute for good, hard, comprehensive physical practice, you still need the mental conditioning to enhance your response and keep you alert in more mundane circumstances.

Mental conditioning requires you to practice in as realistic a situation as possible. Draw on your own experience, or that of others, as scenarios for mental exercises.

The one emotion you can't conceive is the one that makes the greatest difference in a real threat — FEAR. Unlike fights on television, real confrontations aren't logical, patterned, give-and-take brawls. They are a flurry of hitting and screaming, kicking and shoving. You must mentally train for the attack that is certain to be sudden, vicious, and perhaps overwhelming.

2.10 Kinds of Reactions

Confrontational opponents can be categorized by their way of thinking. So can we. The bully is mechanical. He intimidates by brute strength. But the guy who thinks about what he's doing is intellectual. He's unpredictable.

When someone grabs the gun on your right hip, handgun retention teaches you to secure the gun in the holster with your left hand, cock your right arm and CHOP to the rear as you turn to the right. That gets the guy's hand off your gun — fast. But I know one cop who lost his gun by not applying the technique effectively.

That officer was wearing a security style holster. Had he turned to the left instead, the grabber's hand would have forced the trigger guard back under the shroud retaining the gun, as the officer's left forearm chopped the guy's head off.

Now I'm not saying one procedure is better than the other. Both can be correct. The one that *works* is the right one.

While you must repeat the mechanical routines time and again to make them habitual, you must never hesitate to change your strategy to accommodate the situation. Situations aren't scripted, they develop minute to minute, in an infinite variety. If you practiced parrying the pipe swung by a right hander, you'd better be flexible enough to switch if the guy's left-handed.

2.11 Plan

When a situation first presents itself, your mental conditioning is anticipating the subject's first move and planning a countermove by positioning, blocking, or attacking. Your mind runs like a machine gun, thinking of all the possible moves he might make and how you would respond.

But what do you do next?

Focusing on the most probable attack he might make, you counter; and then you should be thinking two or three steps ahead so you have an alternative, should your first attempt fail.

The prevailing mentality today is much as it is portrayed in cowboy movies. The marshal waits for the bad guy to draw first. We wait to be attacked before we can defend. If this guy is challenging us and threatens a grievous assault, why wait? Surprise him. Gain the initiative and prevent his assault. It might convince him his challenge was a bad idea. If it doesn't, you've got him at a disadvantage. You've taken the initiative away from him. You've let him know that *you* have the advantage.

Make him realize the risk to HIM of pursuing his aggressive behavior. Human behaviorists call it "risk aversion." When someone recognizes the high risk of doing something, he avoids doing it.

2.12 Objective

The objective of all this is for you to realize that violent confrontations and personal defense involve more than just the physical element. You need a *mental* awareness of every aspect. Training, applied successfully in real life, builds confidence. And confidence enhances your ability to handle whatever challenge is put to you by an adversary.

3

The Continuum of Force

We keep hearing of civil lawsuits brought against officers for alleged "excessive use of force." These cases are decided by judges who weren't there when it happened. There are likely plenty of witnesses who are happy to testify against the police, so your understanding of "force" is critical to your career.

You are justified in using *only* that force necessary to do what your badge requires you to do.

3.1 Minimum Force

"Force" can be anything. At the bottom of the ladder, your very presence on a scene is a forceful influence. The way you stand (project your image) can influence a situation. Put your hands on your hips and stick your nose in the air and you exude dominance. Stand relaxed, chin down, and you appear supportive. When you say something to a suspect, you are exercising oral control, a form of force depending on your tone of voice.

Verbal force begins with your request to a subject. It progresses to an order, then to an ORDER! Finally, you explain the consequences if the subject doesn't comply with your polite demands.

These are successive rungs as you work your way up the ladder of force.

3.2 Intermediate Force

When you touch a subject, you get into the next level of force that begins with unarmed defensive control techniques. This can be a very unobtrusive grab of the guy's arm that appears passive but gives you a measure of control, such as walking a suspect from a position of advantage. It can escalate to a pain compliance technique, such as a wrist- or thumb-lock.

Higher up the ladder, but still classed as "intermediate," are the impact weapons. Your weapon may be as passive as a short stick on your key ring but, when you know how to use it, it may enable you to control someone much stronger than you. The baton is seen by the public as a standard of police equipment, from a 26-inch stick you carry on patrol to the 36-inch riot baton that looks even more threatening. The PR-24, a side-handle baton, is used on all the television shows because it is more effective than a straight baton.

Nonlethal weapons include a variety of chemical agents and electronic devices that obviously escalate the level of force until the deadly threat response of deadly force reaches the outer limit.

3.3 Deadly Force

When lethal force is justified, you think first of your gun. That's the usual response to a deadly threat. But consider this: *any* force you apply that results in death is deadly force.

If you smash a scumbag's head with your baton and he dies from a brain concussion, that's deadly force. If you apply a bar arm choke hold on a struggling suspect and he suffocates, that's deadly force. The term "deadly force" really refers to the *result* rather than the implement.

Different devices are perceived differently. Your baton is considered "nonlethal," even though you can easily kill someone with it. Your gun is considered "lethal," even though only one in five police shootings result in death.

3.4 Appropriate Force

You need to be concerned with the application of appropriate force because you *will* have to explain your actions in court, sooner or later. With the number of "excessive use of force" suits being brought nowadays, it's a good bet that you will have to justify whatever level of force you used to a judge or jurists who've never been in a fight.

Invariably, "reasonable force" is the concept upon which the court will judge a complaint. According to police trainer Massad Ayoob, "the judgment of the reasonable man" is a standard of the American legal system. Each case is decided on its own extenuating circumstances.

Therefore, properly presented truth is your strongest weapon in court.

Remember that the objectives of your use of force are to achieve and maintain *control*. So your force response must be appropriate to the level of resistance or aggression exerted against you. If a subject curses you with a foul mouth and you zap him with a stun gun to punish him, that's excessive force. If you tell him in an authoritative voice to get into the back seat of your cruiser and he just stands there, your level of force is ineffective and puts you in jeopardy of losing control of the situation.

You are justified in using *only* that force necessary to resolve the situation. If a subject is cooperative, you are justified in giving him directions. If he resists passively, you may be justified in using a mild pain compliance technique. If he actively resists in a defensive manner, you might go to an impact weapon, but used only to apply pressure. If he is aggressive but unarmed, your impact tool may be used more forcefully. If he puts life and limb in jeopardy, your gun may be the only way to stop him.

To put it another way, if a person appears cooperative, you may PERSUADE BY COMMUNICATING. If he doesn't respond to verbal direction, or resists in a defensive manner, you may SEEK COMPLIANCE BY USING UNARMED TACTICS. If he may harm others, or your unarmed tactics have been ineffective, you may IMPEDE BY USING THE BATON. If he threatens death or grievous bodily harm to you or another, you may have to STOP HIM BY USING DEADLY FORCE.

But who makes that decision? The term "deadly force decision" is a misnomer. You don't decide to shoot. You don't decide what level of force to use. Your use of force is in response to the situation presented to you by the subject. Thus, *the subject* determines the type and level of force that is appropriate to resolve the situation. And that's how you need to explain your actions in court.

Remember, the police officer is never the aggressor in a confrontation. "But, your honor, his escalating aggressiveness required me to respond with increasingly higher levels of force." Or, "His actions *compelled* me to use my baton to subdue him."

3.5 Discretion

There's a big difference between "backing off" and "backing down."

If it's been a year since your last in-service defensive tactics training, you may not remember how to get the subject into a control hold. You may have practiced one tactic more than others. The subject could be so big, burly and boisterous that your rusty skills aren't going to work.

You don't want the subject to get the idea that you are ineffective.

If you know the subject to be a skilled fighter with an aggressive personality, you can figure that you might have to escalate to deadly force to resolve the situation. In circumstances like these, it makes more sense to back off and try to defuse the situation—providing it doesn't expose others to injury.

If you are facing a deadly force situation with no chance of winning, you'd be stupid to proceed. "Fools rush in where angels fear to tread" is trite, but true.

When you can't control a subject or situation, you can de-escalate your response. You can disengage and step back, move to cover to wait for backup. Then you become a trained witness, reporting information, noting details and descriptions.

4

Body Language
Speaks Louder Than Words

An officer and his partner had separated the combatants in the domestic dispute. The husband and wife were beginning to settle down when a third officer arrived on the scene. He entered the room with his baton in one hand striking the open palm of his other hand. "What's the problem here?" he asked.

And the fight started all over again.

"When you communicate with a subject, 85 to 90 percent of the message we deliver to people is nonverbal. Only 10 to 15 percent of your message is transmitted verbally," says Roland Ouellette of the Connecticut Law Enforcement Training Institute.

In his one-day course on Management of Aggressive Behavior for unarmed security officers, Ouellette spends nearly as much time on body language, verbalization, and alternatives to physical conflict, as he does on control techniques. His two-day course for police officers includes control techniques, blocking techniques, disarming, and weapon defenses.

"We're in a 35-year crime epidemic," Ouellette says. "Some three percent of Americans 12 years and older will be victims of crime each year; rape, robbery, assault, murder. And the victims are the elderly, women, children, handicapped, the weak, and those perceived to be weak by the assailant."

It stands to reason. The mugger picks his victims by such subtle signs as the way a person walks. If a wimpy looking guy walks furtively with his shoulders slumped and his eyes on the ground, he looks like a victim. If he strolls confidently erect, shoulders back, and looks straight at the potential mugger, the mugger might decide to wait for an easier target. Without saying a word, a person imparts a distinct impression about his vulnerability to someone looking for those signs.

30

The police officer is just as efficient in imparting this information as anyone else. But he can learn to use this phenomenon to his advantage.

4.1 Personal Space

Did you ever notice when a second person joins someone in an elevator, the two will divide the space equally? If a third person enters, they will share the space in thirds. Let someone enter a nearly full car but face to the rear, toward all the people, and they feel uncomfortable.

"That's because your personal space extends farther to the front than it does to the rear," Ouellette says.

Every individual is circled by three rings of a size distinctive to that individual. For the policeman, the outermost is the Alert Zone. Next is the Defense Zone, an area in which an invader puts you on the defensive. The innermost ring, about arm's length plus one hand, is the Attack Zone in which an invader is likely to incite a reaction. A civilian might call these zones Social, Personal, and Intimate. This works both ways.

When you are dealing with a citizen in a verbal situation, stay out of his attack zone. Don't invade his body space, because you may well precipitate his aggression against you. If you're that close, you are vulnerable.

You've seen pictures of the Marine drill sergeant. He intimidates the recruit by moving in close. Notice also his stance.

4.2 Stance

The Marine drill sergeant tries to tower over the poor trainee. His hands are on his hips. His shoulders are back. His chin is raised. His voice is loud and commanding. All these characteristics are gestures that send signals of *aggression*. This may be just how you want to appear when dealing with some scumbag who just snatched an old lady's purse.

If you are trying to calm a combative citizen, would you act like a Marine drill sergeant? Of course not. Such body language would likely prompt him to commit a crime against you. How much better it would be to calm him by appearing supportive, interested in finding out what his problem is, and wanting to help solve it. Assume a supportive stance and you win the citizen's support.

4.2.1 Eye Contact

When you are talking and stare the subject right in the eyes, you are telling him that you are the powerful authority. If you are trying to elicit his cooperation, a direct stare is not likely to motivate him to be your friend.

But if you drop your gaze down to about his sternum, you reduce the power role and become more of a helpful ally.

It works just opposite if you are listening to his story. Looking him straight in the eye makes you appear interested in what he's saying. You are paying attention. If you look off in the distance, or avoid his eyes, you appear disinterested. The citizen could take offense at "his" police department not caring what happened to him.

4.2.2 Posture

Jack Benny made a fortune appearing interested in what Mary Livingston or Rochester was saying. Just look at his posture. Though he was standing, his shoulders were forward, chin down, eyes down, his right hand on his chin with its elbow cradled in his other hand. He appeared very supportive of the person who was talking.

World War II Italian dictator Benito Mussolini, on the other hand, stood with his arms folded, chin up, and shoulders back, as he glared down his nose at the multitude below the balcony. He *looked* so authoritative he was unapproachable. The partisans killed him, then hanged him upside down.

From these visual images you can see the difference in the message you send if your head is back or bowed, chin up or down, shoulders back or forward, arm folded or open. In each case, the first is authoritative and the second is supportive.

When you approach a strange dog you gently offer the back of your hand for him to sniff. Why the back of the hand? Extending your hand palm up is a "stop" signal to a dog or a motorist. It appears authoritative. Yes, it's also a medieval salute to show your opponent that you are unarmed. But, otherwise, the palm is intimidating, the back of the hand is not.

When your teacher scolded you, her finger was pointed or poked at your nose. She was authoritative. The smart guy on the street corner stands with one leg rigid, the other bent. He's trying to look "cool," intimidating everyone who passes.

4.3 Defensibility

Now think back over all these gestures and postures. Expanding the body into a rigid, erect stand elicits hostile response. Contracting the body, relaxing, bowing the head, stooping the shoulders, standing oblique, usually is effective in forestalling violence. But there is another important consideration.

If Mussolini were standing right in front of you, you could have the heel of your hand into the point of his nose before he'd have a chance to sneeze. But if it were Jack Benny standing there as you threw a punch, his pensive arm could quickly extend to parry your blow. In general, the supportive postures put you in a much better defensive position than the authoritative stances.

Anything that works to your advantage is worth trying.

5

Oral Control

One of the policeman's most used but least trained weapons is his voice. Do you ever go into any situation without saying something? Of course not. Communication is fundamental to all you do. And verbalization is a force by which you exercise control.

Writer Richard Garrison tells two stories to prove the point.

A rookie had completed his riding with an FTO (field training officer). He had graduated from the academy. He knew it all, naturally. But during his first shift on his own, he was dispatched to "unknown trouble" at a local market. He found people milling around when he arrived and, in his best command voice, he asked what was happening. A bystander pointed to a subject slipping into the crowd and said something about the subject causing trouble.

The rookie called to the subject, "Excuse me, uh, hey you, uh, I want to . . . We got a complaint of . . ." He got rattled when he couldn't define the complaint.

The subject paid no attention, of course. The rookie caught up with him and grabbed him by the shoulder. The subject, more than a little drunk and angry, turned with a knife in his hand and slashed at the officer. The blade sliced his jacket, glanced off his body armor and cut his forearm.

In another case, officers responded to a domestic disturbance at an apartment house, where a number of family members stood arguing in the front yard. Neighbors were leaning out their windows. The officers separated the most agitated combatants. Suddenly one officer and a subject began to scuffle. The subject broke free and ran with the officer in pursuit. Cornered by a fence, the subject turned and a shot rang out. The subject dropped, wounded in the leg.

The officer said he struggled with the subject over a handgun the man had in his belt. When the subject ran, then turned to point the weapon at the officer, the officer fired.

A weapon was found where the man fell, but no one had seen it before the shooting. The family said the man never owned a gun. A BATF (Bureau of Alcohol, Tobacco and Firearms) trace proved negative.

Witnesses said they saw the struggle, but didn't hear the officer say anything. They simply saw the officer chase the subject, draw his weapon and fire. They said they saw no weapon, other than the officer's.

There are two very different lessons in these examples.

5.1 A Command Voice

The Marine drill instructor demonstrates that short, loud commands elicit quick obedience. You don't call your dog with, "Hey, sweet doggie, would you come here, please?" You call his name to get his attention, then tell him what you want him to do, "Fido, come." Dogs have a limited vocabulary. A person under stress will focus on the few action words. All that polite verbiage is superfluous and counterproductive.

Words that begin with a hard consonant, an explosive rush of air, are more effective than those with a soft sound. "Stop" is better than "Halt." "Don't move" is better than "Stand still." At the NYCPD Firearms and Tactics Training facility there are signs on every wall that say, "POLICE. DON'T MOVE." Three little words that accomplish two purposes.

First is identification. A word that establishes your identity and authority. Say it even if you're in uniform. The suspect and witnesses may be looking somewhere else. Put the accent on the first syllable "PO-LICE" and emphasize the explosive breath of the "P." That helps to get their attention. I'd say "PO-LICE" even if I were a Special Agent of the United States Drug Enforcement Administration.

Second is a terse, loud, lawful command that people are predisposed to obey. If you're walking among the rocks on a sunny summer day and your buddy hollers, "Don't move," you freeze in your tracks, even if you didn't hear the rattle of that snake just two steps ahead. Try a simple test. Ask your wife to slap you on the cheek. She's probably wanted to anyway. But as her hand starts to swing, holler "STOP!" I'll bet you her hand hesitates. When we were toddlers, we learned to obey those short, loud, one-word commands from our mothers.

The policeman must project his voice to be heard the way an actor does on stage. When you holler "Police!" your abdominal muscles should contract to push air from the bottom of your lungs. Talking from the diaphragm, the stage actor calls it. It adds volume and distance to your voice with surprisingly little extra effort.

In the first example, had the officer hollered "STOP!" perhaps the man would have stopped. And the officer would not have been slashed.

When interviewing offenders, Garrison found that the officer with a good bearing, and who seemed to know what he was doing, was the one they did not try to resist or evade. The officer who was hesitant or uncertain, as was the officer in the example, is the one they ignore, escape from, or even attack.

5.2 Extending Commands

Once you've identified yourself and have the subject stopped, tell him what you want him to do next.

In the second example, the officer said nothing. Witnesses heard nothing. Suppose the officer had hollered "STOP!" Perhaps he would have, perhaps not. But if the officer had added three more little words—DROP THAT WEAPON!—it would have helped to establish the fact that the subject was armed, even if the witnesses didn't see the gun.

In any case, the U.S. Supreme Court specifically states in the Garner v. Tennessee decision that verbal commands must be given, wherever practical.

This same decision also negates the threat "Stop or I'll Shoot." Scumbag knows very well that you can't shoot if he isn't threatening anybody. An empty threat makes you look foolish if he calls your bluff. Or he might take your threat seriously and turn on you with a gun so you have to shoot. Then witnesses heard you threaten the subject with violence before you assaulted him. Is it any wonder that empty threats aren't in your best interest?

If the situation is such that you have your gun in your hand, it's better to explain to the suspect, "Don't do anything that would force me to shoot you."

5.3 Giving Commands

Continuing up the continuum of force, your response is determined by what the suspect does. But how can he be compliant if he doesn't know what you want him to do?

Tell him in a few, hard consonant words what you want him to do. "Put your hands up!" "Drop to the ground! Face down." "Show me your hands! Slowly." "Turn around!" "Face the wall."

If he complies, these commands get the suspect into a controlled and safe position. They establish that you are in control.

If he doesn't comply, reinforce the commands with a "Do it now!" in a loud voice. Notice that your commands are positive rather than negative. The positive action word "Stop" is more effective than a negative command "Don't do it."

If he still doesn't comply, you step up to the next rung on the ladder of force.

As you escalate your use of force, however, don't forget to keep talking. When you apply a pain compliance technique, for example, saying, "Cooperate with me and there'll be no pain," may ease his resistance.

Good communications has achieved great purposes. Lack of communications has led to dire consequences. As a matter of fact, that's just what I said to my wife the other day.

6

Verbal Strategies and Tactics

Daniel Vega was walking down a street in Chicago. He spotted a fellow down the block who he thought was acting strangely. The fellow's glances directed Vega's attention to the other side of the street, where there was another man who acted as if he were aware of the other fellow.

As Vega approached the first fellow, he saw the tiny earphone, confirming that he was an undercover cop. The cop greeted Vega in a social tone, explaining, "I'm a Chicago police officer and I think the man I'm tailing suspects I'm on him. Would you please act like you know me?"

Vega and the policeman carried on a conversation. The suspect, reassured, moved around the corner and met his cohort in crime.

"Thank you very much," the officer said, as he moved on.

6.1 Communication Is Key

That sounds like a strange way to begin a discussion of verbal strategies but we're really talking about communications, and communication doesn't have to be loud.

"It's really a matter of understanding people and communicating effectively," Vega says, "You might avoid a conflict with gentle persuasion. If a conflict develops, you can, at least, show justification for your escalation of force."

When the officer approaches a situation he'll see signs that can tell him a lot before he asks the first question.

When the subject sees you, if he's standing relaxed, hands open, unconcerned about your approach, it indicates that he can be dealt with politely. If he's obviously tense, fists clinched, and he backs up as you near him, he's showing fear. You can use that to your advantage. Watch for escape routes, know that you'll have to keep a greater distance to avoid violating the person's personal space, make a decision whether it's better to let him run or to escalate force to restrain the suspect.

If the person is agitated, you need to calm him down before the situation is aggravated. If he hides his hands, leans forward, muscles tense, fists clinched, it's a good sign he's going to attack. Too, an officer can project an image as easily as he can spot one.

6.2 Verbal Skills Work

Is verbalization skills a proper subject for police study? A vulnerable group in dealing with problem people are corrections officers. The policeman can deal with a person and walk away. The corrections officer will deal with that person again, and again.

Vega regularly teaches his Verbal Strategies and Tactics system at the Milwaukee County Sheriff's Academy. Since Vega began this training, violence in the jail has decreased.

"We must be doing something right," he observes.

This process of body language puts a perspective on police interaction. It defines a decision-making rationale that can be explained later in court. For example, say you've had previous contact with a subject. He's usually calm and cool but this time his fists are clinched, he doesn't want to talk, seems to be looking for a way out. You must decide if you want to approach and search him. Is it justified? Or should you keep your distance and observe while keeping your guard up?

You can show him your palms (that's a reassuring gesture) and talk calmly. He will then decide if he wants to go along with you, or try to outfox you.

You've heard the advice to think out a tactical plan while you're responding to a call. Think about what you'll say in that situation as well.

"The important thing here is to have plan A, and plan B. You need to be flexible in your response," Vega says. "Anyone can become violent, for his own reasons that you are unaware of. You must be prepared to deal with any situation that arises.

"That's why complacency kills. This call may not be just like the last one. Be observant to any changes from the last time you were there."

To calm a subject, keep out of his body space, keep your hands open, and speak in a calm tone of voice.

If you can get him to open up verbally, he's less likely to get angry and react violently. Use the opportunity to get information about him, about the

When he's trying to calm a subject, Corrections Officer Todd Ashworth of the Milwaukee County House of Corrections shows him his empty hands; but like this, not like the authoritarian "stop" signal. (David Patrick photo)

situation. But don't give him too much information about yourself. When he starts breathing easier, his anxiety is being relieved.

"If you can get the guy to talk, that's the most effective way to influence someone because you learn his agenda and needs," Vega explains.

6.3 Talk Needed at Every Level

Verbalization is not just one rung of the ladder. It extends all the way through the force continuum. If you had to become more assertive to win the subject's compliance, then you can ease off verbally and keep the confrontation cool. If you had to handcuff him, or use a pain compliance technique, you've proved your point that you are in control. Now try to act more supportive. Give him an opportunity to cooperate.

This avoids making him resentful — a threat just waiting to get even.

Verbalization is important when you're applying a pain compliance technique. Talk to the subject. Explain how he can relieve the pain by complying with your polite request. Tell him what you want him to do, because he will focus on the pain, not on deciding what to do.

Even when you resort to impact weapons or firearms, TALK: "Stop! Don't make me hurt you. Drop that weapon!" These are all commands that will ease the situation, if they work. They also tell any witness within earshot that the guy is armed.

Part of verbalization is letting your partner know what you are doing, what you want him to do. If you mess up and lose control of an aggressive subject's arm, he needs to *know* that.

6.4 Debriefing

Verbalization doesn't end with the arrest. Debrief the suspect. "Are you all right? I notice you hit your head. Do you need a doctor?"

This gives you time to get your own head together, to catch your breath, and regain control of your own physical self. By that time, you probably have an audience. These questions demonstrate to witnesses your concern for the subject's well-being — and they can testify to that fact.

Dr. Parsons, who wrote the foreword to this book, refers to the four D's: Dialogue, Direction, Debriefing and Documentation. Once you've accomplished your goal and made the arrest, document your actions throughout the event. Cite the subject's actions that required you to employ whatever reactions you used.

When facing a crisis in a highly excited state, it's human nature to clam up. But your mouth is the one weapon you always have with you, and use more than any other piece of police equipment.

7

Understanding Control

I've watched as many karate and Kung Fu movies as most people and find them fascinating. They make good "theater." But if you are trying to apply a physical technique to control a subject, theater doesn't count. You need to understand how and why these techniques work. That way, you will be more effective in applying them.

John C. Desmedt is Supervisor of Defensive Measures for the U.S. Secret Service. But more than simply teaching techniques, John conducts a copyrighted class called "Principles of Control" that demonstrates to you *why* the techniques work. His course includes biomechanics, cognitive psychology (high-stress situations) and use of force. We can talk all day but what lets you apply his principles to your technique is actually going through his exercises. Attending his class proved that to me.

7.1 Center of Gravity

Your "center" is where you are. Actually, your center of gravity changes continually as your body position and posture changes, but the mechanical position remains the same.

"The natural point at which your body is perfectly balanced can be pictured as a point about two to four inches below the navel, depending on body size," Desmedt explains.

Drop an imaginary plumb bob down from your center and that spot on the ground is where you "are."

Go ahead. Prove it to yourself. In the interview position, try to shift your weight from one foot to the other—without moving your feet or hips. You can't. But if you move your center by moving your hips, you can complete this exercise easily.

7.2 Physical Stability

Desmedt explains that, being aware of this center, you can use it to your advantage. He paired up the class in teams of two to do some simple tests that prove these principles.

Your partner does the pushing. He stands facing the same direction you are, but turned slightly toward you. He extends his inside hand so the little finger edge touches your breastbone. Now, you stand with your legs about shoulder-width apart in a stiff military stance and tense your body. As the tester gradually increases pressure to your chest, it doesn't take much to push you over backwards.

Now, do the same thing again but, this time, relax your upper body, put most of your weight on the balls of your feet, bend your knees slightly, and lean slightly forward at the waist, so your face is over your center. As pressure is applied to your chest, mentally send the force directly to your center and absorb it there.

The tester had to push with much more force to make his partner move backwards.

"When you tense your body, you become less stable," Desmedt explained.

This center works whether you are standing or moving. To prove it, Desmedt had us walk past the tester. First he told us to think "behind," as if we were being followed. Then we did it again, concentrating on moving our head past the tester's outstretched arm. We were stopped easily each time.

"Do it again, only this time think of moving your center forward to a point several feet past the tester," Desmedt instructed. "Don't concern yourself with the tester, or his arm. Simply walk your center forward to the point you want to reach."

Not only did the tester fail to stop us, some of the guys dragged their testers forward.

Then Desmedt capped it off by having the tester retract his arm at the last second, or not raise his arm at all.

"If you are affected by any of the tester's actions, you are not moving from the center," he explained. "If you mentally bring your coordination point to your upper body, you will be less stable."

7.3 Strength Is in the Center

When you lift a heavy object, you get close and lift with your legs. If you were to bend over and try to lift it with your outstretched arms, you couldn't — or you might break your back. The closer to the center, the stronger you are.

A simple exercise showed this. One partner stood with his arm straight out to the side, his hand in a fist. The other could easily pull the fist down by pulling on the fist. At the forearm, it takes more effort. At the elbow, it's very difficult. At the shoulder, it's next to impossible.

Next, one man stood with his arm straight out in front, hand in a fist. His partner easily pushed the hand aside. They tried again with the fist halfway back to the shoulder, with the elbow against the hip, and with the fist itself against the hip. It was increasingly more difficult to deflect the hand.

"The closer your hands and elbows are to your hips when performing control techniques," Desmedt explained, "the more stable your techniques will be, and the more body power you can use."

7.4 Extension of Power

The power of the mind is awesome. We came to realize that when Desmedt talked about extending power from your center to the opponent. This requires a mental picture, and we got it in another set of tests.

One man stood as if he were aiming a pistol with one hand — fist extended toward the target, arm straight, but elbow not locked. Using both hands, the tester pulled down on the elbow as he pushed up on the wrist. With equally matched partners, the arm bent easily.

"Now," said Desmedt, "open your hand, extend a relaxed arm, and concentrate on sending power from the center, up and through the body, through the arm, and out of the straight, extended, and spread fingers. The direction in which the fingers are pointing is the direction of the power. Guide the power toward a distant object and concentrate on extending it from the center, rather than on the test being performed."

The effect was amazing. As the tester gradually increased pressure, he found it difficult to bend the arm further.

"If you should switch your concentration to the test or contract the muscles of your arm, your arm will bend as easily as it did in the first test," said Desmedt.

"Through this process," he continued, "you are coordinating your brain with the center of your mechanical structure. However, you can concentrate on only one thing at a time, although you can switch your object of attention quickly."

7.5 Focus of Attention

Desmedt demonstrated this focus of attention by having a student stand in front of him with hands clasped on his shoulders. Try as he might, he couldn't lift them off his shoulders by grasping the man's wrists.

Suddenly he slapped the man's left arm and immediately lifted the right arm away. He distracted the "computer" in his head by making it focus attention on an apparent attack. You really can't think of two things at once.

7.6 Momentum Transfer

Stand facing a wall with your forearms vertical, nearly touching it. Push the wall away with your palms and you move backwards. The wall won't move.

Now, stand with your arms straight out but not fully extended, with your palms almost touching the wall. Extend power from your center as you did in the bent-arm exercise. Move your center forward, maintaining that relaxed, unbendable arm. The wall didn't move, but you didn't push yourself backwards, either. Using your body as one coordinated unit, rather than as separate parts performing an uncoordinated effort, gives you power you didn't know you had.

"Pushing without coordination of mind and body may well push yourself off-center and off-balance," Desmedt explained. "Push with mind and body coordinated and you increase your stability, by moving from your natural center of power and movement."

7.7 Energy "Sink"

Ripley's "Believe it or Not" once showed a straight straw that penetrated a telephone pole in a hurricane. A straight structure transfers force directly. But if that straw were bent, it would break.

Stand with your arm straight out, feet wider than shoulder-width, your palm positioned as if signaling "stop." Your arm is straight, elbow locked. When your partner pushes your palm, all of his force goes straight to you and he pushes you over easily.

Do the same thing again; only this time, bend the elbow and extend your power from your center. The tester requires much more energy to move you rearward. The bend is a "sink" that drains off the energy of the push.

7.8 It Works!

Had Desmedt preached a lecture, I'm sure these physical principles would have sailed over the heads of everyone in our class. But *experiencing* these exercises brought the points home. You don't have to be a physicist to understand that:

1. Balance is the basis of power.
2. The closer the center to the support base, the greater the stability.
3. Move one part of a rigid body and the whole body moves. Relax, and the energy is diverted through the center to the ground.

I wish this explanation were enough to make you an expert. These principles can influence everything you learn in defensive tactics. In fact, I think Desmedt's Principles of Control course should be prerequisite for a Defensive Tactics Instructor rating.

8

Restraints and Come Alongs

In a confrontation, the people you face are in one of three frames of mind.

The "yes" person is compliant. He shows you his driver's license when you ask for it. He gets out of his car when you tell him to. Or, he drops his gun when you've got him covered. He's cooperative, whether he's happy about it or not.

The "no" person resists, tells you to commit an unnatural act on yourself, takes a combative stance, and indicates he's going to fight. You must deal with him using techniques to be discussed later.

Then there's the "maybe" person. He hasn't made up his mind what he's going to do. He's the passive resister. He's debating with himself whether to comply or fight or run. The compliance holds we'll talk about here are applicable to the "maybe" person. They may be used when you feel you have an advantage in size, strength, skill, or backup support. They're intended to help convince the subject to do what *you* want him to do.

8.1 Blanket Hold

If the subject is passive, your first grip is to "lay hands gently on," as Gary Klugiewicz says (we'll talk more with him in "Active Countermeasures"). Grasp his right elbow with both your hands, thumbs up. Most people are right-handed. It's safer if two officers each take one of his arms; but if you're alone, odds are his right is his strong side.

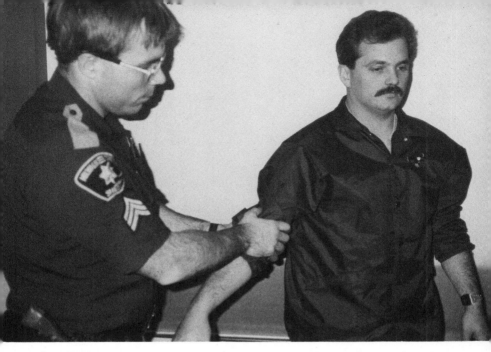

Gary Klugiewicz demonstrates the "blanket hold" that provides surprising control over the subject's arm. (David Patrick photo)

This is a gentle grasp, but it gives you good control of that arm. He can't elbow you or backhand you. If he tries to run at that point, you slip into the escort position.

8.2 Escort Position

Slide your right hand down to the suspect's wrist and get a good pincer grip between your thumb and middle finger. The opposing thumb and middle finger is the strongest grip of the hand. Bring his hand close to your center, as you continue the grip on his elbow.

There are variations of the escort position. Some recommend twisting his hand under, so the back of his hand is against your hip, and hooking your other thumb under his armpit. Some don't recommend this because the subject may drop his shoulder down from your left hand or, if he's double-jointed, bend his elbow. In any case, you lose control.

Let's say you're holding the guy's arm, your left hand on his elbow and your right hand locking his wrist. Say he starts serious resistance. Quickly bend forward with force, and what do you think happens to the subject? He goes forward. But let him to the ground gently. You don't want to write all those long reports to explain his injuries.

Notice that this scenario gives you a sequence of events, explained in your

This is Klugiewicz's "escort" position—wrist and elbow. (David Patrick photo)

If the subject resists, you can simply bend over and bring him to the ground. (David Patrick photo)

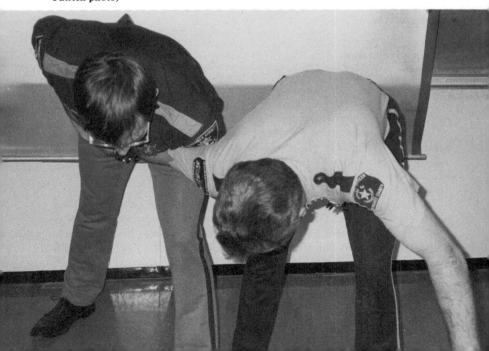

report as justification for using increasingly forceful measures. Control is not a 50-50 proposition. It's all or nothing. If you have half control, you have *no* control.

While this escalation is happening, keep telling him in a stentorian voice, "Sir, calm down. Don't hurt yourself. Stop resisting. Drop the knife. Don't make me do this." Should he grab your holstered gun, when you chop, shout, "SIR, LET GO THE GUN!" Your explosive verbalization adds force to your chop, and lets witnesses know he threatened you.

If you lose control, duck behind him where he can't reach you. Then create distance, so you can draw your baton or gun.

8.3 Come Along

There are many variations applied with both your hands, one hand, or a baton; but they all boil down to one simple principle: anchor his elbow and bend his wrist—the common wrist lock. Any way you can anchor his elbow and bend his hand down with your force against his knuckles, you've got control.

I've seen it applied many ways, but the fundamental point is to jam his elbow into your lower chest, grab his hand and bend it down. Depending on

When the situation gets more serious, this common wrist-lock can be applied either standing . . .

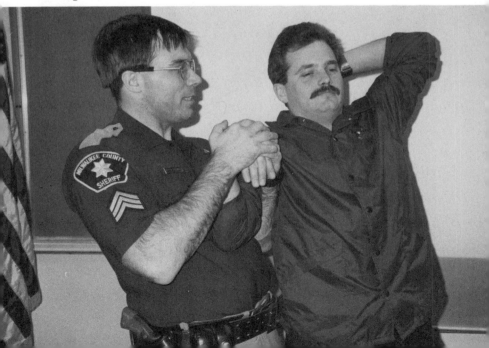

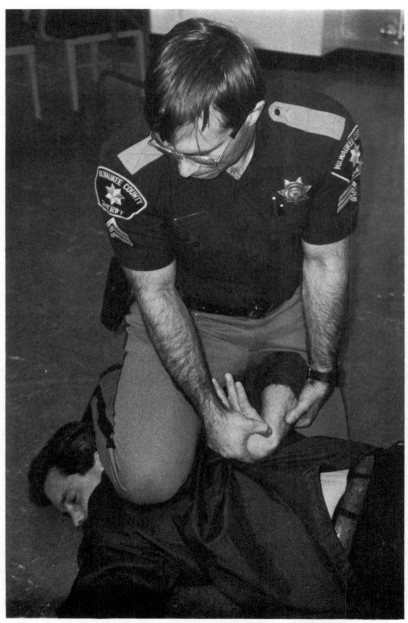

. . . or when you've got him on the ground. (David Patrick photos)

the pressure you exert, it's a come along or pain compliance technique to "stabilize" a person and encourage his cooperation.

The point is that it's part of an overall system, steps along the continuum of force, that can flow from a gentle touch to excruciating pain, depending on the resistance or aggression exerted by the subject.

If he fights, aggressively resists, and you have a subject in a common wrist lock, he becomes a "no" person and more forceful measures are needed. You need to take him down. Just squat — forcefully. You're dropping all your weight on his shoulder and he's going down. You are "directing" him to the ground, as you explain in court — not smashing his face into the gravel.

The come along suddenly becomes a takedown technique.

8.4 Pressure-Point Control

An anatomy book shows you many points on the body where nerves, bones and muscular hollows are so situated that they are vulnerable. These are points to which many of the defensive techniques with a short stick or baton are directed. But some are vulnerable to your hand.

Bruce Siddle of PPCT Management Systems has probably studied pressure-point control more than anyone. What he can do to you with what appears to be a simple grab is astonishing. This could be quite a technical medical subject but he makes it simple — something you and I can do.

8.5 Touch Pressure Points

When I was a kid, I learned to grab that muscle leading from your shoulder to your neck with my fingers. I'd put my fingers or thumb into the depression above the collarbone and opposing digits on the other side, and squeeze. There are many places where a forceful touch can induce pain — on the inside of the upper arm between the biceps and triceps muscles, for example. Other vulnerable spots are described in other chapters, so I won't go into detail here.

Touch pressure points are best used on "maybe" people, so they are a form of come along. If you can't get his wrist, a one-hand hold at a touch pressure point may do the trick.

You can demonstrate the key to touch pressure points on yourself. Touch your temple and push. Nothing happens. Now, use the *tip* of your finger rather than the pad. More concentrated. Now, stabilize your head by putting your other hand on the other side of your head as you push with your fingertip. Next, instead of just holding your head, squeeze your two hands together. See the difference?

8.6 Three Points for Quick Penetration

When a subject actively resists, you need to grab a point that quickly convinces him to do what you ask. There are many potential points of vulnerability, but what can you grab in a fight? What can you get quickly and surely? And how many different holds are you going to remember? To satisfy these questions, the experts emphasize three accessible points.

8.6.1 Behind the Ear

Under the ear lobe, at the top of the jaw hinge, is a depression. Hook your thumb tip into that depression and push up toward the face. You can wrap your fingers over a person's nose to provide a pincer grip to help.

If you drop your thumb a bit lower, you can induce more pain. But that grip is harder to get. With the ear lobe and nose to index your grip, it's quick. So go with the one that's more likely to be successful.

8.6.2 Beneath the Jaw

A jawbone is a U-shaped thing. There's a lot going on back under the middle of your chin. But between the tongue and the jawbone is an area where you can stick your fingertips and induce pain by pressing up toward the nerves at the base of your tongue.

A passive sit-in blocks the public entrance. You have to move the resister. Hook your fingers with the powerful middle fingertip in front of the back angle of his jaw, just inside his jawbone, and lift. It's like scooping butter, and will bring the subject to his feet.

8.6.3 Base of the Neck

Where the neck meets the shoulder, above the collarbone, is another depression where your fingertip may convince a subject to comply with your polite request.

8.7 Motor Points for Striking

Siddle's PPCT system avoids striking joints, such as elbows and knees, with the baton. There is less likelihood of damage and a high probability for effect if you strike motor points. Medical research has identified many areas of the body where nerves are clustered under a thin layer of muscle but over bone to "back up" a strike. Everybody knows about the "funny bone."

There are points in about a four-inch circle on the inside and outside of the thigh, at the top of the calf, on the upper forearm and inside the forearm. Striking these areas with your fist, flashlight, or baton causes a temporary

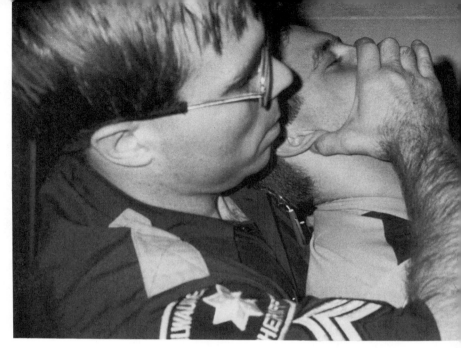

The touch pressure point under the ear lobe is quick and easy. The fingers over the suspect's nose enhances the pressure applied by the tip of the thumb. (David Patrick photo)

motor dysfunction (like hitting your funny bone) that incapacitates the subject for a few seconds, giving you an opportunity to cuff him.

If motor points don't work, you can always aim for the traditional joints. But you can tell the judge that you tried to subdue him humanely before you smashed his knee.

8.8 Pain Is Relative

Touch pressure points, used forcefully, are a type of pain compliance; but different people have different tolerances for pain. A subject high on drugs may not even feel pain. Your pain compliance technique may not work. When it fails, by definition, he is no longer a "maybe" person. He's a "no" person that requires force higher up the continuum — and you can explain why you had to use a higher level of force to gain compliance.

9

Active Countermeasures

Active countermeasures is a system of control techniques that provides the missing link between violent resistance and control. It extends to either extreme of the force continuum, but it's a convenient title under which to discuss a variety of unarmed defensive and control techniques.

Sgt. Gary Klugiewicz, Defensive Tactics Coordinator for the Milwaukee County, Wisconsin, Sheriff's Department Recruit Training Academy, is nationally known for his Active Countermeasures course. It's part of the R.I.S.C. (Rapid, Intense, Specific, Competencies) program adopted by the State of Wisconsin for all police officers. Many other agency instructors have been trained in Gary's techniques.

His course is taught by demonstration, explanation and repetition—realistic simulations—as he puts students through the exercises and drills that make students well practiced in performing these techniques.

Realistic simulation is important. If you received some defensive tactics training in the academy, didn't the instructor warn you about breaking your partner's fingers? And do you think your partner is dumb enough to really resist your efforts? You had to hold back. You indicated where you'd strike with the baton, rather than actually striking. The minute your partner felt pain, he slapped twice—the universal martial arts signal to stop. The techniques you were learning could potentially do damage to the person on whom you applied them.

Officer Guy A. Rossi is an adjunct instructor at the Regional Criminal Justice and Public Safety Training Center in Rochester, New York. He's an

A class in Active Countermeasures is well protected because techniques are applied "for real." The student literally has to fight his way out of a bad scene.

instructor in Active Countermeasures. He's a patrol officer with the Irondequoit Police. So he speaks from experience when he says, "If training wasn't real to begin with, does it come as a surprise when the tactic fails on the street?"

The first time I saw Klugiewicz's seminar on Active Countermeasures, with the participants padded better than a football lineman, I decided it was time for me to shoot some photographs. But the difference between really applying a technique and going through the motions is surprising.

9.1 Decentralizations

In court, you refer to "decentralizing" the subject. "Takedown" is cop talk. When a subject actively resists or attacks, he's not cooperating, is he? He's a "no" person. He isn't going to voluntarily assume a handcuffing position. You have to put him there.

Like most defensive tactics, there are many different techniques, variations on a theme. But a takedown—decentralization, that is—must provide for the safety of the subject, by protecting his head and neck and controlling the speed of descent. It's got to work when you do it fast or slow. Grabbing a subject's hair or head and twisting him to the ground may give you control of his head, but what does that move do to his neck? Whiplash.

An obnoxious drunk would be "directed" to the ground more carefully and slower than someone trying to smash your face. But you still must know how to do it right. If you do a full body slam on a guy, smash his face into the concrete so hard he breaks his neck and dies, the court will call it deadly force. That opens a whole new can of worms in justifying your actions.

These techniques must also be practical. The classic rearward takedown is probably still being taught. But a study in Wisconsin found that it wasn't being used on the street. It might work when done fast, but it didn't work when done slowly. They threw it out of the curriculum.

Now the R.I.S.C. program teaches one basic principle that satisfies the requirements and works from whatever grip you've got on the guy. You can apply it hard or soft, fast or slow. You can stop halfway for his safety, when the subject's off balance.

It's simply bringing the subject to your center and bending over as if you were reaching for your right foot with your left hand, assuming you've got his right arm.

It's that simple. But you won't gain confidence by reading about it. Like learning any motor skill, you have to *do* it.

9.2 Three Levels

The secret of delivering a forceful blow is to translate force through fluid shock waves to motor points of the body. A punch, for example, doesn't stop on contact.

To demonstrate, Klugiewicz had me hold my left arm out and hit the mound of my forearm with my right open hand. It looked like a karate chop, retracting immediately. "Everybody hits like that," Gary said. "There's no power. It's like they say 'Give me back all my power.' This time secure your arm by putting it on the table, and hit it again, but let it sink in."

What a difference. My arm *hurt*.

A boxing parallel might be the difference between a jab and a punch. Rather than pulling back, you imagine the target a bit beyond where your fist hits. You want to transfer the kinetic energy from your hand through fluid shock waves to the subject's internal functions. It's the same principle with a bullet, or a baton.

9.2.1 Stunning Technique

When someone grapples with you, that's an assault. Remember to call it an assault. Can you strike him? Of course. But the guy is hyped-up, drunk, emotionally upset. If you punch him once in the head, it likely won't do any good. You need to divert his attention, take away his ability to resist.

"I 'direct' him to a wall, squad car, tree, bridge abutment—any hard object," Klugiewicz explains.

When someone slams into a hard object, it creates a dysfunction. It can knock the wind out of him. When someone hits backwards into a wall, it's really a spread out diffused strike, disrupting the synapses of the brain.

You can prove it yourself. Stand about four inches from the wall and ask your wife to push you forcefully backwards. When the back of your shoulders hits the wall, your eyes stutter and you feel quite shaken up.

With one undamaging blow you have accomplished more than multiple blows with your portable radio or baton could have produced.

"We found that many officers have done this instinctively," Klugiewicz says. "And you can do it vertically or horizontally with a much lower propensity for damage."

9.2.2 Diffused Strike

Using these fluid shock waves to cause trauma on the body, you can addle a subject without really hurting him. If you break his bones, you'll have to write a long report. So, you want to hit the places where it won't do heavy-duty damage.

The diffused strike can be a stunning blow without propensity for damage. (David Patrick photo)

Klugiewicz laid the inside of his forearm at the base of my neck, the same place we discussed in pressure point control. Then he pulled his arm out six to eight inches and slammed it back with modest force. That was enough to cause me some discomfort.

"This diffused strike is like a mobile wall stun," he explained.

It's not like a chop-and-retract that does little, or punching "through" that winds up pushing the subject backwards. It's a relaxed boom that lets everything rest into the subject. When you do it right, you can feel the vibration in the subject's body. It's comparable to the energy dump of an expanding bullet going into ballistic gelatin.

"You don't need a lot of techniques or a high skill level if you learn to hit properly using fluid shock waves," Klugiewicz added.

9.2.3 Unarmed Blocking and Striking

When the guy attacks, your ready-position is like the boxer's stance — hands up by your face, elbows tucked in. Swing side to side to guard against chest attacks. If he swings high, pop your arm up, block, and retract. Abdominal strikes can be deflected by dropping your elbow. If he swings low, swoop your arm down, around and back up.

But don't just stand there and box with the guy. Your purpose is to decide the confrontation as quickly as possible. One block is all you should ever need. Once you've blocked his attack, you counterattack with a hand or leg strike, wrist lock, diffused strike, baton, or gun — whatever is called for.

A vertical punch to the suspect's jaw (like a left jab with the fist held vertically) stops his forward momentum, makes him bring his hands up and sets him up for a reverse punch (like a strong-right punch) to the lower abdomen to stun him. Then you can direct him to the ground and cuff him, effecting the arrest with a minimum amount of force.

Besides your fists, you might block or strike with your forearm, front or back side of the elbow, knee or foot. A front kick aimed at his lower abdomen might keep him away. If he's already too close, it's a knee into his abdomen. That'll do it, every time.

9.3 Purposes

Active countermeasures are what you use when you have to. They're for when you need to regain lost control, or can't reach your baton or firearm. Countermeasures can give you the opportunity to grab your baton or gun if the situation calls for it. And they give you a "weapon" to use when the situation no longer is appropriate for impact weapons.

They can defend you against an assault. They can distract the assailant. They can stun the subject to disorient him. They can impede him when his legs are knocked out from under him. They can stop his attack. They can enable

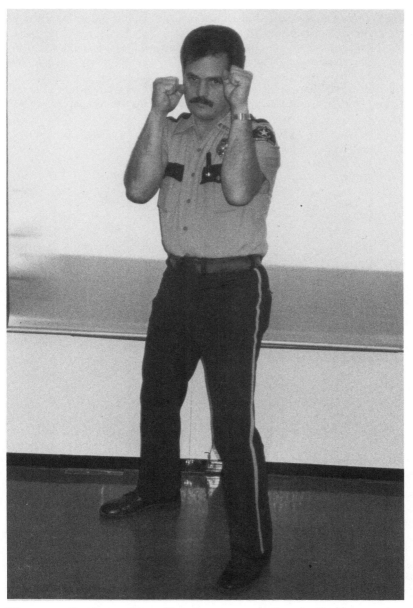

When an assailant lunges, this position gives you more options for blocking, parrying, and striking. (David Patrick photo)

you to control an aggressive subject and manage him into a position where he can no longer threaten you.

I was surprised how few fundamental principles Klugiewicz employs in his Active Countermeasures system. And how many ways those few principles can be used to defend yourself.

"We don't want multiple techniques that you won't remember," he explains. "We want multiple applications of a few effective techniques you will remember."

10

Neck Restraints

When you are facing a husky adversary, especially if he's bigger than you, it requires *technique* to restrain him, rather than brute strength. There have been enough martial arts movies to show us that a slightly built black belt can do what he wants with a Man Mountain Dean. Now, I can guarantee you I'll never become a black belt. But I can become so well trained, and so well practiced, that even a boisterous bruiser would have a hard time taking me down — despite the gray hair.

I mention this now because I saw a film of a 125-pound female police officer restrain, take down, and cuff a 210-pound construction worker using the Lateral Vascular Neck Restraint, developed by Jim Lindell of the Regional Police Training Academy of the Kansas City, Missouri, Police Department.

No, we're not talking about the old choke hold.

10.1 Danger of Bar Arm Hold

With all the publicity given to liability suits lost after a perpetrator died as a result of being restrained by a choke hold, only a reminder should be needed. But, incredibly, I hear that some policemen are still being taught the bar arm hold. Let this word to the wise be sufficient: *Never use a bar arm choke hold.*

A bar across the front of a subject's neck — whether it's your forearm, flashlight, or baton — can damage his windpipe, break the hyoid bone (Adam's apple), crush the larynx (voice box), and bring dire consequences to both him and you. You are justified in using only the degree of force necessary to effect the arrest. If the guy dies, you used DEADLY force, whether you meant to or not. Good intentions are nice, but courts deal in facts.

When an aggressor gets his arm around your neck, you get your chin into the crook of his elbow immediately. You are avoiding a bar arm and protecting your airway. You must do the same thing when you apply a neck restraint on someone else.

10.2 Carotid Restraint

In the film I mentioned, the dainty policewoman reduced the burly bruiser's height with a kick into the backs of his knees. Then she got her arm around the guy's neck — all the way around. Her elbow was in front and her hand extended back behind the guy's shoulder. Her other hand came up and clasped that hand, palms together with fingers wrapped, not interlaced. Then she pulled.

Her hip hit the guy's butt, broke his balance to the rear and she had him under control.

10.2.1 How It Works

This restraint works by the scissors effect of your biceps and forearm bearing on either side of the subject's neck. When you squeeze the two together, it hurts. The carotid arteries run up the sides of the neck carrying a blood supply to the brain, so you have to be careful.

The way this technique is generally taught, it is NOT the "sleeper" hold of judo. But its severity can be increased if you're not careful. When Jim Lindell of the Kansas City PD was demonstrating the technique at a defensive tactics seminar, he raised his elbow with his arm around a student's neck and explained how that increases the hold's effectiveness. But he cut short his talk as he lowered the officer, who was out like a light, to the mat.

It was generally accepted that restriction of oxygenated blood to the brain was caused by compressing the carotid arteries. But a new theory has been advanced by Dr. James Cooper of St. Louis, Missouri. He's a vascular surgeon, who believes that four physiological factors work in combination: venous compression, vagus nerve stimulation, some carotid compression, and the Valsalva Maneuver.

The Lateral Vascular Neck Restraint is effective and safe when its purpose and function are thoroughly understood, and the technique is properly used by the officer. In most situations, it should be used *only* as a last resort before physical violence.

It can be applied from any position, right- or left-handed. It's adaptable to exert varying degrees of force. And it can be relaxed immediately when resistance ceases.

While you should practice using the technique from both right and left sides, a right-handed officer is well advised to favor using his left arm around the subject's neck. This puts his gun side away from the suspect and his right hand can be quickly freed if he should need it.

10.2.2 Technique

If you're standing in the interview position, your weak side is already toward the subject. When he starts resisting your best efforts, step to his left side, curl your left arm around his neck, and break his balance to the rear. Your arm should be far enough around his neck to put your elbow directly in front. Your hand extends back behind his shoulder with the palm down. The subject's airway is protected and he can breathe normally. Your biceps is against the left side of his neck and your lower forearm is against his other.

Bring your right hand up, palm up, and clasp the palms together. Wrap the fingers of each hand around the other. This allows the pull of the right hand to help exert pressure against the sides of the neck. Try lacing your fingers and see if you can pull hard against your left hand. Your hands come apart. With a handshake clasp, you can exert a lot of pull.

The lateral vascular neck restraint puts a subject off balance, so you can let him down to the floor easily if you want.

At the same time, place the side of your head above the ear against the back of the subject's head. This helps to increase pressure forward and prevents any attempt by the subject to butt you.

As this is happening, take a step or two to the rear. Keep your knees bent and legs widespread to help you maintain balance. This unbalances the subject and he can't use his leg, waist, or shoulder strength to continue his resistance. You can keep him under control as long as his balance is broken rearward.

10.2.3 Degrees of Control

Mild Restraint is often enough. What we've discussed so far puts the subject off balance with your arm loosely around his neck. It can help break up fights, keep combatants separated, restrain a suspect on the scene, and it just may convince a resister that he can be controlled.

Medium Restraint may be needed if resistance continues. Now you compress his neck between your biceps and forearm and you can pull with the back hand to put on more pressure. You can cause him pain. If it's your left arm around his neck, raise your right elbow a bit and notice how much that adds to the neck pressure. This should be enough to control all but the most violent resistance, and it shows the resister that he is firmly restrained.

Maximum Restraint should be used *only* if all else fails. The subject is held firmly by the neck and his balance is broken to the rear. Pressure is increased against the sides of his neck by your left arm biceps, pulling back with the right arm, and elevating your right elbow more. It's at this point that you have to be careful. IMMEDIATELY RELAX AS SOON AS RESISTANCE CEASES. If the subject loses consciousness, ease him gently down your forward leg to the ground, taking care to protect his head.

Notice that this isn't a "sleeper" hold at the stages you would normally use it. But it can quickly be turned into one by increasing pressure and elevating your rear elbow, if it comes to that.

10.3 Safety

While there are many kinds of neck restraints, Lindell limits his teaching to this one Two-Arm Carotid Restraint. It is the safest for the subject at all levels of control, and it provides the officer with a sequence of one application that can be adapted to different situations.

As long as you can clasp your hands behind the subject's back, you can be sure that the arm is properly positioned on the sides of the neck. If you have to reach to the side of the subject's neck, your forearm may be forming a bar across his throat. Only with proper arm position can you break his balance with the same encircling action as you step to the rear, and maintain a safe distance between you and the subject as you maintain control.

A properly applied neck restraint can have the effect of protecting the subject's neck from injury. Your arm and head act like a cervical collar preventing lateral movement. When your head presses against the back of his head, your arm positioned under his chin allows only enough pressure to control backward movement, but not enough to move his head forward.

"When you have this 'neck brace,' you know you've applied the restraint properly and achieved the safe and protective potential inherent in its correct use," Lindell says.

10.4 Medical Concerns

If you should ever render a subject unconscious, immediate relaxation should revive him in five to 20 seconds without any help from you. Loosen his collar and tie to aid his normal breathing.

In the off chance he doesn't revive in 30 seconds, start approved methods of resuscitation *immediately* as a precaution.

If a subject has been rendered unconscious, when he revives he should be informed that medical attention is available to him and, if he asks for it, he should be taken to a medical facility.

10.5 Legal Concerns

The question has been raised in several states, "Does the carotid neck restraint constitute 'deadly force'?" The answer is cloudy.

You now know the difference between the lateral carotic hold and the frontal bar arm hold. But they look a lot alike. The Minnesota POST Board researched the legal aspect and found two relevant cases.

The first case reached the U.S. Supreme Court, City of Los Angeles vs. Lyons, 103 S.Ct. 1660 (1983). Lyons sought to enjoin the Los Angeles Police Department from using the neck restraint in the future. The court denied the injunction because, it said, Lyons could not prove that he was likely to be subjected to the technique again. But the court characterized the hold as "use of deadly force" and implied that Lyons might have been successful had he sued the city for damages.

McQurter vs. City of Atlanta, 572 F. Supp. 1401 (D Ga. 1983) came out of a federal district court. McQurter had resisted being handcuffed. One of the officers used his flashlight in a choke hold to the front of his throat and subdued him while other officers cuffed him. There was testimony indicating that once he was manacled, there was no possibility of McQurter's escape. But the officer then shifted his position to the safer carotid neck restraint, tightening when the subject struggled and relaxing when he quit. For fifteen minutes before the wagon arrived, McQurter was motionless, apparently unconscious. No one checked him. He was taken to a hospital and put in the detention area. It was some time before hospital personnel noticed anything wrong with him. He was dead.

The court held that once he was cuffed, further use of the neck restraint was unnecessary. Then the court said, "no one could have believed that the USE OF DEADLY FORCE was necessary to prevent an escape, death, or serious bodily harm." The city, superiors and four officers at the scene were held liable for showing deliberate indifference to the serious medical needs of the subject.

Those who teach the carotid neck restraint caution against excessive application. They know the difference between "restraint" and "deadly force." But history proves that people have died from a bar arm choke hold that looks a lot like a carotid neck restraint — and judges and juries paint with a broad brush. Now there is legal precedent that naively lumps a safe control technique in with one that has caused death.

You should be aware of this concern but, as for me, I'm more concerned with my own well being at the time of the scuffle. And the Lateral Vascular Neck Restraint might save my skin without having to resort to impact weapons.

11

Yawara in Police Service

Yawara, as an art, dates back to 17th century Japan. Jujitsu schools of that time included the short stick among its weapons with tactics so fierce it became known as "seven inches of sudden death."

Such severe martial arts tactics and weapons have no place in police service. But a form of Yawara has become popular among officers who know how to use it.

Frank A. Matsuyama was looking for an alternative for the traditional sap and billy. His Yawara was a seven-inch piece of plastic, 1¼ inches in diameter. The ends were rounded with four metal spikes embedded near the tip and butt. Grooves aided gripping while the spikes discouraged adversaries from trying to grab it.

Most Yawaras today are made either with rounded ends or with a steel ball on each end. More than a dozen varying designs have been popular over the years, although all have a relatively thick grip limiting them to thrusting, striking, or blocking techniques.

Dr. Kevin Parsons, in his book *Techniques of Vigilance* (1980, Charles E. Tuttle Co., $35), says the Police Yawara was popular on the West Coast in the early 1950s.

A variety of Yawara sticks sold to police include the first Yawara with its original manual, at far left. Next, left to right, is the original Monadnock model (still made); the Kel Lite Judo Stick (discontinued); Monadnock's first Chemical Yawara; Monadnock's most popular model; and Jim Morrell's Mo Gem (which contains a flashlight).

11.1 Carrying the Yawara

Holsters are made for the Yawara and it is best carried just behind your sidearm. Be as selective in your choice of a holster as you are in one for your handgun. Both need to be immediately available when you need them. Which one you reach for depends upon the nature of the resistance or aggression exerted against you by the subject.

11.2 Strikes

Strikes with the Yawara are directed to vulnerable areas of the body and such blows can be devastating. When you hit the temple, base of the skull, or esophagus, the result could be fatal. Use *only* if deadly force is justified.

Strikes to the chest, abdomen, up under the chin, or down into the hollow of the shoulder, are less than lethal but could still cause injury.

Generally considered restricted areas of the body are the head, throat, solar plexus, lower abdomen, groin, spine, and kidneys.

The officer with a Yawara is better advised to use it *only* in defensive techniques.

11.3 Blocks

While advanced Yawara includes many blocking techniques, you are ad-

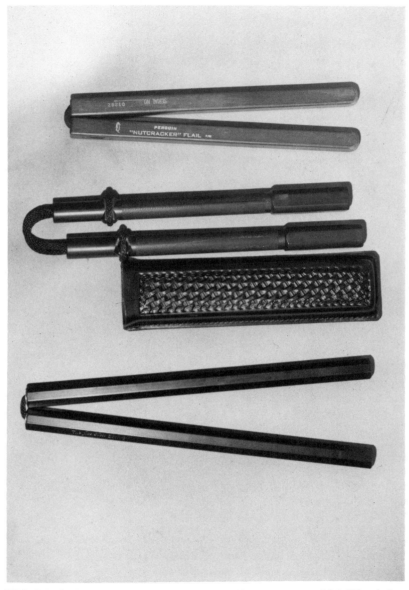

While I don't advocate martial arts weapons for police, there are models of Nunchakus available. From top to bottom: the Penguin Nutcracker Flail (discontinued), Orcutt's Police Nunchaku, and the Joe Hess Backup.

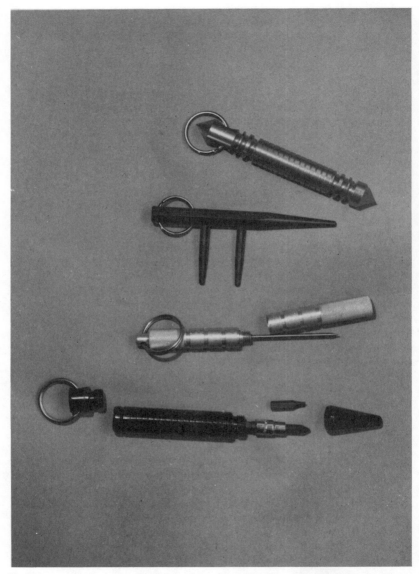

You'd be surprised what's offered for sale to the public. The pointed-end metal stick at top is an oriental import. Below it is the Ninji key chain (those two points stick out between the fingers of your fist). Next down is a knurled stick that unscrews, to reveal an "ice pick." At bottom, the Mugger Hustler, which doubles as a screwdriver with straight or Phillips points.

Here are some more seemingly harmless devices that conceal a weapon. The decorative buckle at the upper left really is a .22 caliber pistol that drops into your hand with the touch of a button. In other devices shown, blades are variously hidden in a belt, key, card case, fountain pen, or bracelet; even the ivory ornament is a knife. The classic switchblade is at right.

vised only to use the palm hold, if you're not a black belt artist. Simply hold it with your strong hand like the grip on a suitcase.

The Yawara really becomes a focus of attention as you block your opponent's wrist with your wrist, his arm with your arm. It gives you something to tighten your fist on, and that makes your blocks more effective.

When blocking, it is important to move your arm in a big, loose circle, tightening into a hard block at the point of impact. According to Dr. Parsons, muscle relaxation increases blocking speed. Tensing the whole body at the point of impact provides stability against the thrust and puts you in position to execute a rapid counterattack.

11.4 Evolution

Even though the policeman may use the Yawara strictly as a defensive weapon, it is seen by the public as a martial arts device. From this, there has evolved a system that can be used with a device that appears less intimidating. That's why I don't call the short stick a "Yawara."

12

Short Stick Techniques

It isn't unusual to put a fob of some kind on your key ring. A short stick is a handy device that you can tuck into your belt and keep the keys safe and accessible. The men's room key at the gasoline station is usually on a stick, so the customers don't lose it.

Why would you want to keep your keys on a short stick?

12.1 A Defensible Defensive Device

When I attended a *Kubotan* instructor course at the S&W Academy, instructor John Peters told the story of an officer who was sued for brutality after taking down a particularly boisterous resister. The judge told the officer to bring the weapon he used into court. When the officer appeared the next day, the judge didn't see anything in his hands and became irritated.

"Where's your weapon?" the judge asked angrily. "Did you bring it?"

"Yes I did, your honor," the officer replied.

"Well, let me see it."

With that, the officer put his key ring on the table. It had a six-inch stick on it, with six grooves apparently providing a grip.

When the officer explained that this indeed was the weapon he used to subdue the aggressor, the judge used colorful language in throwing the case out of court.

70

12.2 The Kubotan

This officer was carrying a *Kubotan*, a trademarked product of Karate Master Takayuki Kubota, who developed these techniques.

Technically, we're not talking about the Yawara, a martial arts weapon. Mail order sales of many martial arts devices are attracting the attention of legislators. They are becoming the subject of prohibitive legislation. But who feels threatened by a key fob? A short stick?

Yet, a trained officer stands a good chance of controlling even an NFL linebacker with a short stick. The assailant who lunges at you quickly finds himself face down on the ground as you cuff his wrists. A determined passive resister suddenly sits up and presents his wrists for cuffing. The driver who gets a death grip on the steering wheel and refuses to get out of the car changes his mind when the stick is applied to his wrist.

12.3 Why It Works

The short stick is a pain compliance device in police use. Bone is living tissue, sheathed in a sensitive membrane. There are a number of points on the body where the bone is close under the skin and pressure against the resistant bone with a hard object produces pain — *plenty of pain*. That's where the short stick comes in.

I've heard stories about a subject who had been severely beaten with a baton, but continued to fight. When a backup officer arrived, he took out his short stick and brought the confrontation to a screeching halt. Four orderlies couldn't control a mental patient, but the policeman they called quickly subdued him with a short stick. Frankly, I'm skeptical of such stories.

The *Mini-Maglite* with my car, garage, and police station keys on it tucks into my belt in front of my revolver. A quick draw can reach whichever is appropriate.

Isolated incidents don't prove a general rule. As with any pain compliance device, someone who is insensitive to pain won't be convinced by your deft application of a short stick. He might not stop even after being shot, unless your bullet hits a vital organ. So, while I carry a *Kubotan*, it isn't an absolute solution. It's an alternative to more severe force and it may work in some situations.

12.4 Six Simple Moves

In the course I took, six basic techniques were taught and they are all variations of two simple moves: a squeeze and a poke.

1. An uncooperative subject needs convincing. Approach with your weak side toward him to keep your gun in safer position, and grab his strong wrist with your weak hand. You've got the stick in your strong hand. Put the stick over his wrist, so it's horizontal, and flip your weak hand thumb up and over the stick on the side away from your strong hand. Squeeze your weak hand as you push down with your strong hand, and the subject decides to do as you ask.

2. A subject reaches to grab your shirt. Sidestep his fist and clamp the stick over his wrist, your fingers around the stick, both of your thumbs under his wrist. Grind the stick into his wrist bones where they're close under the skin by closing your fingers, and step back. The subject willingly goes to the ground.

3. You've told a subject to come with you, but he turns to walk away. As one of his wrists swings rearward, cup it between the thumb and fingers of your weak hand as you push the stick around the inside of his wrist and wrap the fingers of your weak hand around it.

With your thumbs behind the subject's wrist, you've got a vise grip. Step back with your strong foot, forcing him to the ground. Then you can step over him and kneel on his other shoulder while you cuff the wrist you hold.

In these techniques, the stick is most effective when placed against the radial bone. Reach out to shake hands. The bone on top is the radius. Don't let the stick slip around the wrist, because that puts it on a better padded area and relieves the pain.

4. You need to walk the subject so you want a "position of advantage." One technique you'll learn in defensive tactics is grabbing one of his wrists with your same side hand and twisting it to put the back of his hand against your hip as you push your other thumb under his armpit or grasp his elbow. Instead, you can use a short stick poked into the brachial nerve in his upper arm.

Feel your own arm. About half way from elbow to shoulder on the inside you feel a depression below the biceps muscle. There's a bone below with the brachial nerve over it. Holding the stick like a microphone, poke the edge of it there and you can induce pain.

The ulnar nerve runs along the inside of the elbow. Bend the subject's elbow slightly by lifting his wrist and poke the stick into the depression.

Should you need to take the subject down, push with the stick as you pull his wrist back. He readily takes a bow. Quickly slide the stick down his forearm to the base of his thumb and lock your thumb around his. Your weak hand continues to hold his wrist as your weak thumb flips up and over the end of the stick. Pull the stick with your weak thumb toward your strong thumb, as you exert downward pressure. Step back with your strong foot and pull the subject face down on the ground. Step over him, kneel and cuff with your weak hand as your strong hand maintains its grip on the stick. Be careful not to overbend his thumb. You might break it.

5. You're standing in the interview position and you've told the subject he's under arrest. The stick is in your strong hand. He replies, "I'm not going" and just stands there.

Begin with a poke to the hollow of his left shoulder. It's the nearer of the two. Just inside the shoulder joint, below the clavicle, there's a depression. Poke the stick into that depression on the subject as your weak hand grabs his right arm, spinning him around.

This *Kubotan* instructor class practiced techniques; you know the "subject" didn't resist, nor did the "officer" cause undue pain — they switched for the next exercise, so the other partner could get "revenge."

Now, his back is toward you and the stick is still in his shoulder. Turn your strong hand thumb up and continue downward pressure in that shoulder depression. Bring your weak arm up under the subject's armpit and your weak hand can help put on the pressure. Notice that this is not a choke hold.

Downward pressure on the stick will force the subject to bend his knees. As he starts to sit, bring your left hand down to his left wrist and swing his arm down behind his back.

Gently put the subject into a sitting position by sliding him down your strong leg. Pulling his wrist as you push the stick will pivot him against your strong knee and into a face-down prone position. At this point, I prefer a thumb lock; simply clamp the stick around his thumb so you have his thumb between your thumb and the stick. A little pressure convinces him to do what you ask.

Pin his shoulder with your weak knee as you cuff the wrist so willingly presented.

But suppose you're holding the stick in your weak hand when he lunges?

A variation of the above: Sidestep his lunge and poke the stick into the back of his near shoulder (outside of the shoulder blade), as your strong hand pushes his other shoulder. This pivots him around so his back is toward you. Then bring the stick up under his armpit and into the depression in the front of his shoulder. Continue the takedown as already described.

6. The conventional position against a wall or draped over a car isn't always as safe for police as we once thought it was. But there is a way you can do a "stop-and-frisk" right out in the open, all by yourself. In fact, there are a couple of different ways.

One variation is to face the subject away from you with his arms outstretched to the side. With the stick in your strong hand, slide it between the fingers of his strong hand so two are on each side of the stick. Wrap your fingers around his fingers and squeeze. He'll gladly stand still while your weak hand pats him down. Try it on your own fingers and you'll see why.

Another variation: With the subject facing away from you, tell him to put his right hand behind his neck and his weak hand behind his back. Approach with your weak leg forward and slide your weak hand under his weak arm. Put the stick between his fingers and wrap his fingers with your weak hand, palm toward you. It's similar to the wristlock in the Downey-Roth handcuffing technique.

Now, bring the handcuff in your strong hand and push it onto his right wrist. If he resists, squeeze your weak hand around his fingers. Then you can bring his cuffed wrist down behind his back and put the other cuff on his weak wrist.

12.5 Variations

There are any number of ways and situations in which you can apply these basic techniques.

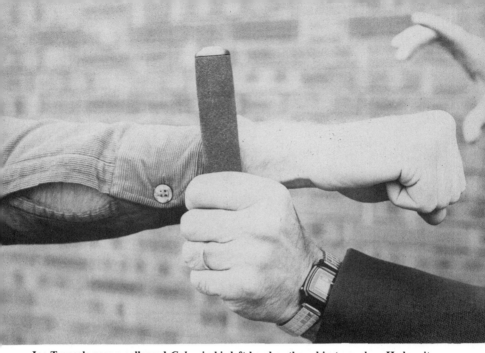

Joe Truncale uses a collapsed *Cobra* in his left hand as the subject punches. He lays it alongside the subject's wrist . . .

then reaches over with his right hand to provide a vise grip that induces pain, and convinces the assailant he had a bad idea. (Truncale photos)

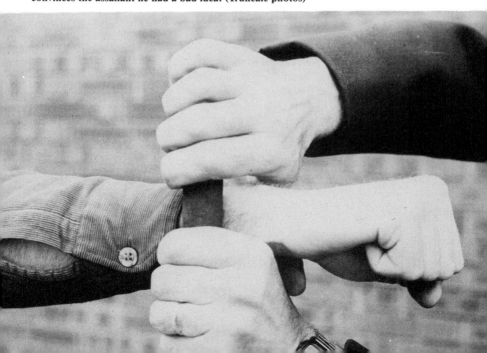

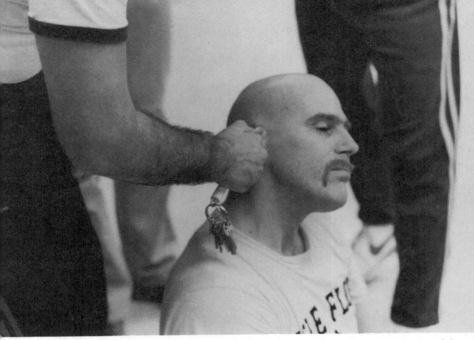

A sit-in refuses to stand? The edge of your *Kubotan* on his ear flap provides powerful lifting motivation.

Protesters often lock their arms and lie down, face up, across the entrance to the defense plant. The edge of the stick under a protester's ear lobe convinces him to sit up.

A motorist gets a death grip on the steering wheel and refuses to get out of his car after you've opened the door. Bring the stick under the driver's left arm and over his wrist, and then lock your thumbs on the underside. Step back as you grind the stick into his radial bone. He'll come with you and gladly lie face-down on the street. Step over him, kneel to pin his shoulder and cuff.

Or you could swing him around to drape him over the trunk of his car to keep him away from passing traffic.

If a wristlock is awkward, grab his left wrist with your weak hand, palm down. Come under his arm and poke the stick into the inside of his elbow or biceps and push. He will fold forward as his arm twists, pointing his thumb up. Then slide the stick down to get a thumb lock.

If the car door is closed and the window is open, apply a wrist hold. Bring that arm through the window as he unsnaps his seat belt with his right hand. Open the door, pulling him partially out of the car. Tell him to put his right arm behind his back and quickly switch the stick to his right wrist. Then he can untangle himself from the car door and move over to the trunk for cuffing.

If a subject is seated, grabbing the edges of his chair, and refuses to budge,

Officer Tom Dumas played the reluctant motorist, until John Peters applied the *Kubotan* to his wrist.

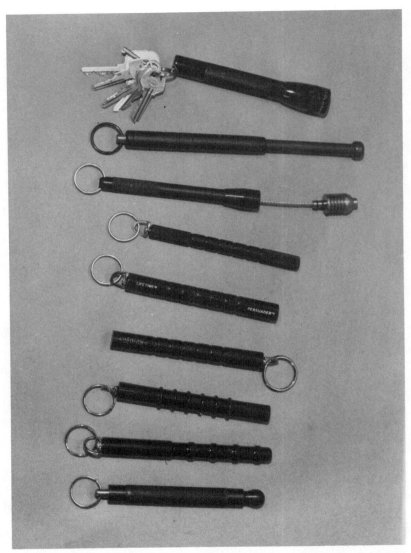

The *Mini-Maglite,* top, is shown with a variety of short sticks on the market. Below, the *P9* from Armament Systems and Procedures is actually an expandable baton; the *Defender* end unscrews to release a length of cable, for use as a twister; next is Monadnock's thin *Persuader*, and its original model *Persuader*; with key ring to right, the *Kubotan*; Monadnock's *Persuader* Model 2 has raised ridges; the *Keyfend* has rounded edges and provides a good grip for flailing keys; at bottom is a metal model with a rounded-ball end.

apply the stick in a wrist clamp and you can bring that arm behind him for cuffing. Or, you can grab his wrist and poke the stick into his brachial or ulnar nerve area (biceps or elbow) as you pull his wrist from the chair seat. Then slide the stick down into a thumb lock. If he's standing latched onto a vertical pipe (or jail cell bars), you can do the same thing.

Suppose the passive protester has folded his arms across his chest so tightly you can't get a wrist clamp. Poke the stick into the back of his hand and he'll move it quickly enough. Then get his wrist in your vise grip.

When you want him to stand up, cup his chin with your weak hand as you poke the stick into his back below the shoulder blade. Push upward with a swooping motion and he'll help you lift him to his feet. Or pinch his ear lobe between your thumb and the edge of the stick.

If someone grabs you in a bear hug from behind, you have several options.

Bounce your bowling ball head into his face. Swing your hip out of the way, as you chop your hand or stick down and back into his groin. If you can't move your upper arms, the pen from your shirt pocket or short stick from your belt poked into the back of his hand encourages him to get his hand away from you. If he gets you in a full nelson hold, you can still reach the back of his hand. As he loosens his grip, swing the stick into his lower abdomen. If he gets you in a choke hold, tuck your chin into the crook of his elbow to protect your airway and poke the stick into the muscles and tendons of his forearm. The short stick isn't an impact weapon, but if it's the only thing in your hand when someone kicks at you, sidestep as you snap it down onto his shin.

If you learn how to use it, the short stick can be a very effective tool in dealing with unarmed combatants. Then, when you are brought into civil court for using excessive force, the judge may think someone's trying to kid him when he sees your key ring.

12.6 Many on the Market

There are more than a dozen short stick devices on the market. Monadnock Lifetime Products produces the *Persuader*, designed by Paul Sterrett. It is similar in size to the *Kubotan*, but with raised ridges rather than grooves. The *Pow-R Stick* is made by the Universal Corporation and was designed by Capt. James Smith. It is made of steel with a key ring on one end. *Keyfend*, also metal, was designed by Stanley Kubas. The *Penfriend*, or *Back-Up*, was designed by Joseph Truncale of the Glenview, Illinois, Police Department, who co-authored the University of Illinois book, *The Police Yawara Stick*.

Truncale is a staff associate at the University of Illinois Police Training Institute. He is well qualified in use of the police Yawara stick. He credits Kubota with developing the shorter and thinner type stick. But Truncale often uses just a six-inch piece of ¾-inch wooden dowel, "which does the job," he says.

13

Proper Use of the Flashlight

The driver pulled his car over to the curb when the siren signaled him to stop. According to testimony, the motorist resisted, scuffled with the two officers who had stopped him, consequently was subdued with their flashlights. The subject later died. The McDuffy case in Miami brought a judgment against the city and, with all of the television network coverage, put police flashlights in a bad light — pun intended.

Obviously, beating someone about the head is not a proper use of the flashlight. It also isn't proper use of the police baton.

13.1 A Touchy Subject

The flashlight in police service is becoming a dichotomy — a necessary piece of police equipment that is falling into such legal disfavor that some chiefs have gone so far as to prohibit the long, aluminum body lights and any training in the proper use of a flashlight. Their theory is that if their officers use only simple flashlights and aren't trained in their proper use, they avoid liability should the flashlight be used to inflict injury.

One major carrier of police insurance charges an additional premium to departments that use flashlights. They are considering a policy to deny insurance to any department that does not prohibit the use of police flashlights.

I'm no lawyer, but I can't see how policemen could be prohibited from using flashlights. A light source is a necessity. If you have a flashlight in your hand when someone jumps you, you've got no choice. Are you going to drop your only light source to grab your baton? Of course not. You'll smash that plastic two-cell, or whatever else is in your hand, into the guy praying to buy time so you can grab a better weapon. That's the way life is.

In my opinion, it is important to be equipped with a light that can do the baton's job, and to be trained in its proper use.

That's an important point the emotional tirades against flashlights seem to overlook. The only difference between a police flashlight and a baton is the light bulb at one end. But no one advocates prohibiting batons. To my mind, any prohibition of police flashlights would have to apply also to police batons *because they can both be used in the same way.*

It's well established that lack of training can incur liability.

If officers are issued a proper flashlight and are trained in its defensive use, the department can show a positive liability defense. It also works in your favor. The principle is the same as with a baton. You are trained never to strike above the shoulders. As long as you use the baton in the manner in which you were trained, you have a defense against civil suit. As long as you use the flashlight in the manner in which you were trained, you should also have a defense. That's logical.

The flashlight is nothing more than a short baton or a big *Kubotan* when it is employed as a defensive device. You'll see that flashlight techniques discussed here are essentially the same as baton or short stick techniques. Misuse any of these devices and you may be liable for using excessive force.

John G. Peters, Jr., president of the Defensive Tactics Institute, likes to say, "Flashlights don't hit people, don't cause courts to award millions in alleged excessive force settlements, nor set policy."

John Peters wrote the book *Defensive Tactics with Flashlights* (Reliapon Police Products, P.O. Box 14872, Station G N.E., Albuquerque, NM 87111, $9.95). It devotes many more pages and illustrations to show the techniques that we'll cover here.

13.2 Flashlight Holds

No one has to tell you how to hold a flashlight "civilian" style. But cops also use a different kind of hold for two reasons. (1) You are looking into a stopped car or dark basement niches so you want to look down the flashlight beam, and (2) you want the light to be "cocked" and ready for defensive use. So the policeman holds his light backwards — with his weak hand, palm up, so that the barrel of the light rests on his shoulder as he aims the beam through the car window.

What follows is meant only to help you understand these defensive techniques. You can't learn them without physical practice under the watchful eyes of a qualified instructor.

Be nice. Give the motorist light to help him find his driver's license. This hold lets you look down the flashlight beam into a car window, as Officer Tom Lapore demonstrates.

13.3 Defensive Techniques

You're holding the flashlight in the normal civilian hold. The suspect swings a piece of pipe at your head. The hand holding the light comes up, laying the barrel of the light along your forearm. The same as with the baton, the light provides a protective shield that takes the brunt of the blow and deflects the attacker's weapon.

If he throws a punch, let his fist hit your light instead of your chin. You can grab the tail end of the light with your other hand and use it like a bar to block the attacker's swing or kick.

When you've practiced defensive techniques with the flashlight, you can parry his fist with the light, sandwich his wrist against the light with your other hand, and have him in a controlling wristlock before he knows it.

Should someone grab your shirt while talking face-to-face, you can use the short stick technique with your thumbs forming a yoke. Or, you can bring the light in your left hand around and over his wrist, so your left hand lies to the right of his wrist. Reach under with your right hand and grab the light to the left of his wrist. Keep your hands as close together as possible and you have his wrist locked into the tiny triangle between the light and your crossed wrists. Then you can take him down, if need be.

The flashlight in Hank Kudlinski's right hand provides a hard surface for the attacker's arm to hit.

Say you're standing in the interview position, holding the light at shoulder height. Should the subject suddenly throw a punch, step back to increase distance and snap the light onto his wrist or forearm. If you're holding the light in your weak hand and he punches with his right fist, you'll hit the outside of his arm. If the light is in your right hand, you'll hit the inside of his arm. But you don't have to deflect his punch by much to make it miss your chin. You could even add your other hand, like on a baseball bat, to add force to your swing.

If he gives you the old one-two, it works better to hit the inside of his striking arm. You may have to swing back the other way to block his opposite arm.

After blocking the punch, you may need to bring the light back to your waist and thrust the end cap into his lower chest area. If he still doesn't stop fighting, flip the head of the light down into his groin.

13.4 Control and Restraint Techniques

Think of your flashlight as a fat *Kubotan*. You can use the short stick techniques to apply restraints and control holds.

You've told him to come with you but he turns to walk away. Remember the *Kubotan* technique? Slip the flashlight around his wrist, grab the light with your other hand and clamp his wrist under your thumbs against the light. Squeeze as you rotate the light with your fingers, and he suddenly becomes quite compliant. Or, you can take him down for cuffing.

Step back as you squeeze the light against his wrist, forcing the subject to lean forward going facedown on the ground. Keeping firm pressure on his radial bone to maintain control, step over his arm and kneel on his shoulder. Your other leg traps his arm. Grabbing his fingers and hyper-extending them raises his wrist for cuffing.

The flashlight adds a measure of control to the arm lock. Standing alongside the subject, grab his right wrist with your left hand. Lift his arm so the elbow bends. Trap his arm by pushing his elbow between your left side and left forearm. Push the light over his arm and under your left triceps. Grab the front of your light with your left hand and you have a control hold that leaves your right hand free. Pulling on the light, as you flex your left arm muscles, helps to convince the subject that he should walk with you without resistance.

13.5 Retention Techniques

Let's go back to the interview position, with the flashlight in your hand in the police hold. Since you're in a lighted area, the light is off. But you gesture, pointing the end cap toward the subject. He grabs it, more than likely with his right hand, toward the tail end of the barrel.

There are several things you can do.

Grabbing what you've got with both hands, rotate your hands and light in a small clockwise motion. The subject's wrist will bend as the tail of the light points upward. Continue the circular motion until the person's hand is palm up. Forcibly push the tail end of the light down against the subject's wrist, prying the light from under his thumb.

Or, you can grab the tail end with your other hand and spin the flashlight like a propeller through the weak point of his grip — his thumb.

Or, you can grab the tail end with your other hand and, as you step forward with your weak side foot, and flip the head of the light down into his groin or stomach.

Or, say he grabs the tail end so you can't. Grab the barrel of the light with your other hand, palm down, so both hands are holding it the same way. Slide your leading hand forward and cover the subject's thumb; then force it into the light. This should cause him enough pain that he'll want to let go. But keep your grip. Forceably point the light downward as you step back, bringing the subject to the ground. Keep his arm straight by pulling upward on the light.

To get him ready for cuffing, walk toward his feet as you keep pulling up on the light. When he's on his stomach, bend his arm at the elbow and kneel on his shoulder, as you maintain the thumblock and apply the handcuffs.

13.6 Caution

There are many variations of the techniques you can apply with your flashlight (or baton). Most instructors I know concentrate their training on just a few techniques that are easy to remember and more natural in their response to a situation. That's fine. But most cops don't get a chance to practice what they learn in too-brief training classes. Why learn complicated martial arts if you're not going to maintain a level of proficiency that makes them work? You need techniques that will happen *naturally* when you need them on the street.

Be careful when you apply any defensive tactics techniques. There's a fine line between pain compliance and a broken bone. That's why you shouldn't read a book, then apply a technique, without being trained by a qualified instructor.

14

Impact Weapons

When Sir Robert Peel established the world's first organized police force in London in 1829, he armed them with truncheons, a stick that carried over into the New World as the police baton. The baton has been part of police equipment ever since there have been policemen. In fact, drawings on cave walls show prehistoric man using a stick of some sort as a weapon.

History classifies the baton as an impact weapon, but the way police use it today, it's not; that is, in the sense of a club with which you bash someone's head. But "impact" is a convenient category in which to discuss several devices. Many have come and gone.

14.1 Historical Devices

The short billy club was the traditional truncheon for police officers in the early days. But it is best suited for an overhand swing onto a person's head. Its range is short if you try to jab with it, and it really isn't long enough for the techniques you learn today.

The blackjack is a lump of lead on a springy handle covered with braided leather. Its flexibility gives it a snapping action that increases the momentum of the blow. It's designed to deliver a knockout blow to someone's head; and that could have dire consequences.

The sap, or slapper, is a lump of lead between two layers of leather. It's more rigid than a blackjack and, theoretically, is less likely to crush a skull. Its effectiveness is in striking bone, such as ankles, shins, or wrists. It's handy for close-in fighting.

You'll find saps still being made and sold — and carried by police officers today. But show one to a judge and what will he think: "Oh, that's what you hit him on the head with." None of these devices are viewed as defensive. On the other hand, your baton is backed with a training program of a variety of techniques for controlling a subject, blocking his attack, or hitting him in places you can't reach with a sap. Its very design shows its suitability for many things — except hitting heads. It's not a club.

You may also find sap gloves for sale where they haven't been banned by police administrators. This is a leather glove with a pad of powdered lead over the knuckles. Frankly, the best use for sap gloves is to protect your hands when using a two-hand riot baton. But the public is likely to put them in the category of brass knuckles — a thug's weapon, not a policeman's.

Palm saps have a similar problem. This is a leather covered pad of lead that covers your palm, with a strap around the back of your hand. A slap in the face with one feels like a hammer blow. But consider that a slap in the face is seen by society as the classic challenge to a duel. How will a judge interpret your slapping a suspect to subdue him?

I classify all of these devices as "historical," because that's where they belong — in history. They are bound to be construed as weapons of aggression,

Police impact weapons: at upper left is an original British bobby's billy from Kevin Parson's collection; below it, to left, is a 40-year-old hard rubber "Metropolitan Police Club." At right, from top down, is a blackjack, palm sap, sap, and Outer's *Gun Stick*.

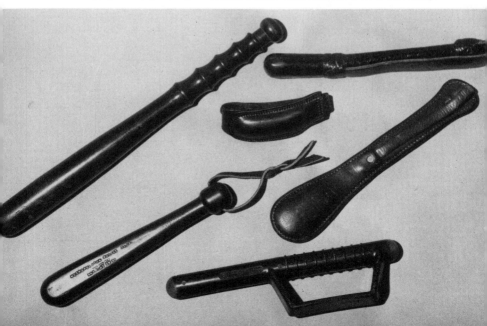

even if you use them defensively, because society sees them as serving no other purpose than to hit with.

After all, the object of your nonlethal force is to gain compliance, to control a combative subject, not to knock him senseless.

Your baton has many uses and your instructor can prove it with his lesson plan. A straight stick is obviously not designed for bashing heads. It's a lever, jabber, blocker, and many other defensive things when you must take it to court.

14.2 Straight Baton

Rolland Ouellette of the Connecticut Law Enforcement Training Institute gave us a quick review of basic techniques with the straight baton when a local labor dispute threatened to erupt into a strike. They are indicative of the many ways you can use a stick defensively.

The right-hander wears his baton on the left, like a sword. With your left hand on the grip, you could punch it straight ahead into an aggressor's abdomen. Or, you could draw it like a sword, if you want to intimidate someone. You can be more subtle by putting your right hand behind your back, using the left hand to lift the baton and push the grip back to your hand, and you've got it where others don't easily see it.

Holding it like a sword puts it into view. It's less intimidating to hold it upside down with the blade up behind your arm. It's hidden, but readily available.

Lift your hand and clasp the baton horizontally under your upper arm, like a riding crop. While it is more visible, this ready position still isn't a threatening presentation of a baton. But you can deliver a devastating blow from this position.

Have your partner hang his stick about three feet in front of you. Slowly, flip your stick forward as you extend your hand, but be careful that you hit his stick and not his hand. Retract your stick after the blow is struck. Speed up your action each time you try this. Get a real flipping motion. The tip of your baton travels a lot faster than your hand. With practice, you might even knock the stick out of your partner's hand.

Also, from that hidden carry position, your baton is ready to block an aggressor's punch, parry the pipe he swings, or stop his kick to your groin.

If he punches at you, simply bring your hand up, with the baton against what is now the outside of your forearm. There's a nice hard surface for his fist to crash into.

Should he swing a piece of pipe with his right hand and you've got your baton in your right hand, bring it across in front of you pushing your left hand at the tip of the baton. The baton is now at a 45-degree angle, grip farther forward than the tip, so his bludgeon glances down your baton and, hopefully,

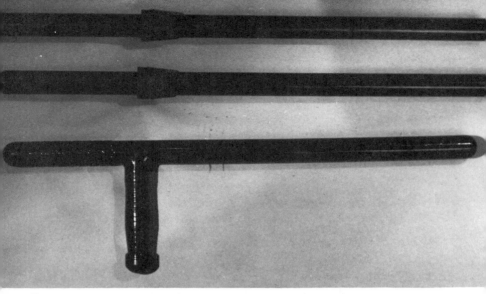

Batons you normally see are, from top to bottom, the standard 26-inch model; one with a metal knob on the end for better jabbing, and the PR-24 side-handle baton.

swings into his own shin. Keep your lower left hand open to keep your fingers out of the way.

If he starts to swing a kick up between your legs, flip the tip of the baton to your other hand and extend your arms. His shin meets the stick before his toe touches your family pride.

You can move a person back by holding the baton sort of like a pool cue, jabbing it through your left hand into his abdomen. But retract it quickly to keep him from grabbing it.

An arm lock is more effective when you put your baton under his wrist and over his upper arm. As you raise the grip, you can increase pain.

You can do the lateral neck restraint with the baton. From the hidden carry position, make a "V" with the stick and your forearm. Whip the baton around his neck, making sure your hand is to his front, so you don't crush his windpipe. Reach behind his neck and grab the tip of your stick. Putting pressure on both sides of his neck, between your baton and your forearm, induces pain.

Obviously, there is much more to baton techniques than this. We're simply showing examples of the different ways it can be used. You're not going to become adept at any of these techniques without actually practicing them under the supervision of a qualified instructor.

14.3 Side-Handle Baton

The side-handle baton, the PR-24 from Monadnock, was developed in 1971 by Lon Anderson. It is everything a straight baton is and more.

Holding the side-handle in the "ready" position, you can jab the short end into a person's abdomen. The block that you can do with a straight baton can be done with the side-handle baton and your hand is out of the way. That flipping strike is really devastating when you spin the side-handle baton, using the handle as a pivot.

The handle gives you leverage, much more so than a straight baton. The baton come along holds are easier to do with the side-handle, providing an extra dimension, like a shepherd's crook. It is so effective that Massad Ayoob, director of the Lethal Force Institute, says, "It is unwise to hold this instrument in other than the ready position, since the handle gives so much leverage that whoever is holding it pretty much has control of the weapon."

Using the side-handle baton is so different from a straight baton that you need specific training and certification before you're allowed to carry it.

14.4 Expandable Baton

Batons are an acceptable and effective tool for the police officer. But what's a plainclothes man to do? It isn't very convenient to conceal a 26-inch stick under your coat. Dr. Kevin Parsons recognized this need and designed an expandable baton he calls the *Cobra*.

There are two models. One goes from 6¼ inches closed to 16¼ inches opened. The other is a nine-inch handle that extends to 26 inches expanded.

The expandable baton has the advantage of appearing less intimidating than a long stick hanging from a ring on your belt. With it collapsed, you can use the *Cobra* to do the short stick techniques. When you need an extended strike, a flip of the wrist extends it, even as you swing.

If you swing overhand, snap your wrist so the baton extends to the front. You can do the same thing if you swing backhand. I don't particularly care for the outward swings to open the *Cobra*, up or to the side, because they leave your baton out of action until you bring it back, but they're handy if an aggressor is toward your right side.

Once opened, the *Cobra* stays open. It's designed to be rigid against a soft surface like a body. You can do the jabs that you would with a straight baton. The *Cobra* has a blunt 7/16-inch tip.

To close it, you have to kneel on the concrete and slam the tip down on a hard surface.

14.5 Targets and Nontargets

There are vulnerable parts of the body you must avoid with any impact weapon. The head and neck are always off limits. Avoid the solar plexus, because a hard strike could cause internal injuries. Kidneys and groin are highly sensitive areas that should not be struck with a hard object. Avoid the spine. From the neck to the tail bone (coccyx), a concentrated blow to the backbone with a baton could cause permanent injury.

Target areas identified by Joe Truncale of Professional Police & Security Systems are the Achilles tendons, the instep, shins, sides of the knee joints, thighs, backs of hands and fingers, wrists, elbows, and lower abdomen—just below the navel. More generally, proper baton targets are grouped in four areas: arms and ribs at elbow height, lower abdomen, forearms and wrists, and sides of the knees.

15

Handcuffing Techniques

This is not the place for a technical evaluation of handcuffs. In 1982, the Technical Assessment Program of the National Institute of Justice reported on tests of 17 models of double-locking handcuffs. Since then, three new models have been tested and found to comply with NIJ Standard 0307.01 for Metallic Handcuffs.

You can get the Consumer Product List and the Metallic Handcuff Testing Report from the NIJ's Technical Assessment Program Information Center (call 1-800-24-TAPIC. In Maryland and metropolitan Washington, D.C., call 301-251-5060).

With this NIJ testing program exposing family secrets, cuff makers have redesigned some of the traditional, highly polished handcuffs. You can imagine my disappointment when my favorite model didn't pass the test. But the ones I carry today look just the same, and they did pass. So not all of this redesign was just to make them cheaper to produce. There was good reason and the benefit is yours.

15.1 Historical Devices

It is interesting, however, to see what devices were developed in past years to give a policeman control of a subject's wrist. Like the historical impact weapons, these also belong to history.

There was the Twister, two interlocking T-shaped handles with a length of chain between. The idea was to get the chain around the guy's wrist, clamp the handles together in your one hand, and you could twist it to induce pain.

The Claw was a bit more expedient to use. One in my collection locks opens and arms a trigger under the shaft to the T-shaped handle. When you push it onto a subject's wrist, the trigger is tripped and the claws clamp shut and you have a handle on the guy's wrist. A twist would force the clamps into the sides of the claw into the sides of his wrist. Another version required you to pull a collar on the shaft to clamp it shut.

But these were not "manacles," as such. You had to occupy one hand with

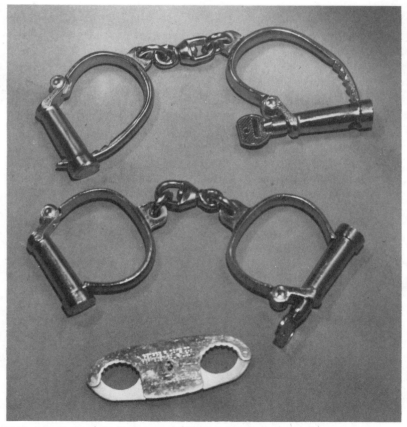

Old handcuffs from the Kevin Parsons collection show variations in designs. The top model clicks through to adjust the size of the loop, while the hook on the cuff below it snaps to lock. Both keys work like a screw to unlock. At bottom are thumb cuffs.

Thumb cuffs literally "handcuff" the thumbs, like this. They're a convenient size but the propensity for injury in a scuffle is obvious.

The *Iron Claw*, on left, could be used with one hand. Once you had the chain around a subject's wrist, the *Twister* (right) let you control him with one hand.

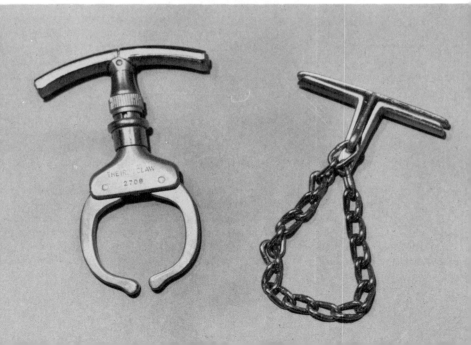

Modern handcuffs include, left to right, the traditional chain, double rigid hinge, and triple hinge.

them. Early "handcuffs" were called "manacles" or "shackles." They left you free of controlling the subject's hands. And that's the purpose of handcuffs — to shackle a subject so he cannot use his hands to fight.

15.2 Modern Types

Smith & Wesson offers a line of traditional chain link handcuffs that comply with NIJ standards. The Model 100 comes in blue or nickel finish. The Model 103 in stainless steel is for humid or salty air environments. The Model 104 is the new maximum security model with a unique new key design. All S&W cuffs weigh 10 ounces.

In addition to the traditional chain link cuffs, Peerless produces a model that is stiff-hinged. The two cuffs are connected with two bicycle chain type of links. They fold to fit your handcuff case, but they don't twist.

Hiatts of England offers a Tri-Hinge model that's as rigid as they come, but folds flat to fit a standard handcuff case. Tri-Hinge models with standard double-lock come in nickel-plated steel #2050, black anodized steel #2075, and nickel-plated lightweight alloy #3050. They also have chain link steel cuffs in anodized black or nickel that weigh 10 ounces — #2015 and #2010, respectively. Their lightweight models weigh just 4.5 ounces, #3000 in satin finish, and

#3010 in nickel. There are also three models with a push-button double lock, #2020 nickel, #2025 black, and #3020 lightweight nickel.

Both the Pearless and Hiatts stiff-hinged cuffs allow a more expedient method of handcuffing a suspect. We'll get into that later.

15.3 Getting Him Ready

Everyone has his favorite technique for handcuffing a suspect. What's best depends on how cooperative the subject is — or isn't. Just remember there are three reasons why policemen are vulnerable while handcuffing a suspect: (1) they get into an unsafe position, (2) they don't have the subject under control, or (3) they relax too soon.

A popular technique that's effective and reasonably safe is the one developed by Robert Downey and Jordan Roth of the California Specialized Training Institute.

If the suspect stops after your command "POLICE, DON'T MOVE," tell him "You're under arrest. RAISE YOUR HANDS HIGH." Immediately assume an alert position at a safe distance. Making him "stretch for the sky" will lift his clothing to reveal weapons tucked into his belt. Even a concealed gun under the tightened shirt should bulge. Order him to turn a full circle SLOWLY, so you get a good look all around.

15.4 Cuffing an Unarmed Suspect

No weapons spotted? Don't count on it. But the ground's muddy so you decide to cuff him standing up.

Command him to spread his feet slightly, put his left hand behind his back, and his right hand behind his neck. (Mirror image for left-handed officers.) Now you can reholster to get your gun out of the way while you approach. Always approach from a different direction than the suspect last saw you, but be extremely alert during the approach. If scumbag flinches, *create distance* as you go for your gun.

Grab the suspect's left elbow and wrist and compress them toward each other. This is a pain compliance hold while you get in position to slip your left arm around his elbow and grab his wrist with your left hand. Now you can control him with your one arm, while your right hand cuffs his right wrist up behind his neck.

Maintaining control of his left wrist, bring his right hand behind his back and cuff his left wrist. Now you can walk him to the car while keeping that wrist or finger lock.

15.5 Cuffing an Armed Suspect

Let's say the suspect fits the description of an armed robber in an area you'd expect him to be after holding up a store. You don't want to take any chances. Because the suspect is considered "armed and dangerous," you need to get him into a controllable situation *immediately*; and you're justified in holding your gun on him.

Position him facing away from you. Tell him to stretch his arms high to raise his clothing and turn to check his waistband. Now, order him to drop to his knees, then to reach his hands to the ground ahead as he crawls backwards to drop face-down flat, arms out to the side, palms up. Make him turn his face away from the direction you plan to approach and spread his feet wide apart, sides of feet flat on the ground. Put your gun back into its security holster before you approach.

Approach from his left side and put your left knee into the nape of his neck. Immediately grab his left wrist and apply a wrist lock. Tell him to put his right wrist behind his back so you can cuff it, then cuff the left wrist.

"Never struggle," says Bob Lindsey, former Captain with the Jefferson Parish (Louisiana) Sheriff's Department. "If he resists and you've lost your control hold, *create distance* for your own sake, and start over."

My department firearms instructor, Frank Starnes, likes a variation of this technique. Once a subject is prone, instead of spreading his feet, command him to raise his feet off the ground and to hook his right foot over his left calf.

Approach from his foot-end, still covering him with your gun, and grab his left toe, as you kneel on his right leg, and push. Now you can reholster and grab the heel with your right hand. Just a little twisting pressure convinces him that you can cause him pain if he doesn't comply. But don't cause such pain that he'll try to get away.

You could do a quick pat down at this point, if you wish. Just be careful twisting his foot. Too much pressure could break his ankle. Command him to put his right hand to his back and cuff it, then do the left hand — keeping some pressure on the toe of that foot to maintain control.

Then you can stand him up and do a proper frisk.

Suppose you find the gun he was reported to have. *Don't* stuff it in the front of your pants. There's not only the potential for a family relations damaging accident, it also keeps the gun within the suspect's reach. If you've got a back-up, hand the gun to him. At least put it behind you, if you're sure it's safe.

15.6 The Wall Is Passé

Capt. George Armbruster of the Lafayette Parish (Louisiana) Sheriff's Department has researched handcuffing techniques extensively. He agrees that the Downey-Roth technique is far superior to the old "assume the position against the wall" approach.

When the subject is leaning against the wall, you don't have him in a control hold. So you hook your left foot around his. He might kick you off

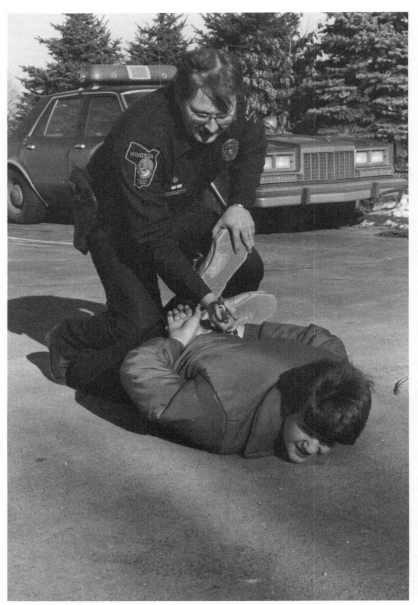

A variation favored by Officer Frank Starnes for potentially dangerous characters is this ankle twist. Police Explorer Jeff Mucha – on the ground – played his role well.

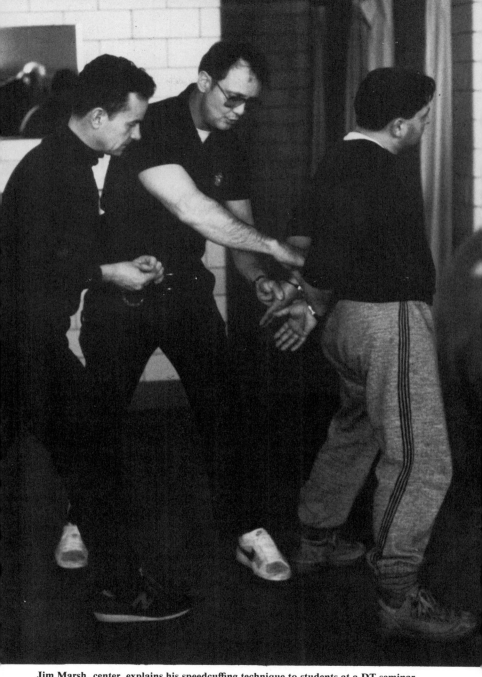

Jim Marsh, center, explains his speedcuffing technique to students at a DT seminar.

balance as easily as you trip him to the ground. He can push off from the stationary object and be in a struggle for your gun before you have a chance to draw.

15.7 Speedcuffing

Jim Marsh of the Chicago Police Department teaches speedcuffing.

First, you "load" the cuffs, pushed nearly all the way through. Grasp them in your right hand with one cuff above and one below your hand, the single-strand facing out. Command the subject to put his arms out to the side, thumbs down, then to bring his hand to his rear. Now you have him standing like a jet plane, thumbs pointing toward the ground, palms toward each other.

Grab his right thumb from underneath (where you can bend it back, if need be) and turn his hand, palm up. Push the top cuff onto his right wrist from the little finger side. Then quickly swing the bottom cuff under his hand as you grab his left thumb. This underhanded swipe clamps the bottom cuff on his left wrist, and he's cuffed in less time than it takes to tell it.

With the rigid-hinge cuffs, another simple and speedy technique is possible. Prepare the subject in the same way and "load" the cuff the same way. Grab the subject's two thumbs together in your left hand as you lay the cuffs, moving parts down, onto his wrists that are properly positioned for you; then just push the cuffs down. Both cuffs engage respective wrists at the same time.

16

Fighting the Knife

Nothing seems as ominous as the flash of a knife in the hands of an angry and irrational person. Perhaps it's the mental picture of your blood gushing from a gaping wound or an eviscerated victim lying *all over* the street. Not even a gun poses such an indecisive threat.

Indecisive? Of course. A crazed hophead with a knife standing 20 feet away from you is no threat. Right? That's the way a jury would see it. I learned just how *wrong* that idea is at a Knife/Counter-Knife course conducted at the Lethal Force Institute (LFI) in Concord, New Hampshire.

16.1 The Knife IS a Threat

The dozen students teamed up in threes. One "victim" stood 20 feet away from the "attacker." The third timed the attacker's lunge with a stop watch. Even the 62-year-old man in class "stabbed" his victim in 1.64 seconds. Younger men all timed less than 1.5 seconds. So?

"Your honor, he may have been 20 feet away but I was only one-and-a-half seconds from death — and I can testify to that fact."

"If you are threatened by a madman with a knife 20 feet away, there's certainly justification for using your gun," said LFI Director Massad Ayoob. "He has the knife for capability, puts you in jeopardy by his words and actions, and the opportunity is only 1.5 seconds away."

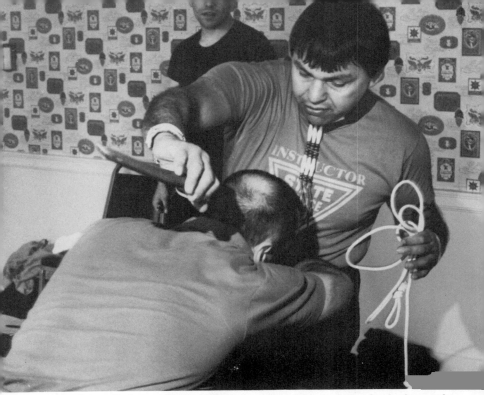

Jim Maloney had swung the "knife," but the student deftly ducked under the threat as he delivered a fist to the attacker's diaphragm.

Fortunately, each "victim" could have gotten off a shot or two before the "attacker's" rubber knife struck. But bullets don't always stop an aggressor. In this situation, you might be better off using a PR-24 baton technique.

"If you've got the PR-24 in your hand, it's quicker than trying to draw your gun," says Rolland Ouelette of the Connecticut Law Enforcement Training Institute.

A New York City Police sergeant and his partner responded to an armed robbery call at a bar. The robber had a knife. The officer approached but kept a "safe" 12-foot distance. The robber lunged, the cop shot twice. But the aggressor still reached the officer, stabbed and killed him before he fell.

Suppose you aren't wearing a gun?

16.2 Using Your Fists

"If you know how to move and how to punch, you can defend yourself against a knife attack," Instructor Jim Maloney told our class. "As the attacker lunges, a proper sidestep makes his thrust miss as you deliver a devastating punch to take him down."

Maloney has survived many such encounters. He grew up on a Micmac Indian reserve outside Halifax, Nova Scotia, where "a lot of harsh living conditions existed, and you were judged on how you could take care of yourself." At 40, Maloney is a fifth-degree black belt in Uechi-Ryu karate. He was chief of the three-man tribal police force before he opened his Special Tactical and Response Academy.

"My brother was chief of the reservation. That helped," he quipped.

Standing five-foot-six and weighing 160 pounds, Maloney doesn't look much like Rambo; but we soon learned differently. One student thrust a rubber knife and, before he could recover, found his knife waving in thin air and Maloney's fist just touching his solar plexus.

With what I learned, given a bit more practice, I'm confident that, if someone attacked me with a knife, I could deflect his thrust, slice his throat and stab him in the heart before he could say, "Oh, s---."

Just learning to hit properly is the difference between a love pat and a bone-crushing blow.

Our class paired up, half using boxer's practice mitts. Maloney demonstrated a straight punch, no windup, no swoop, just a straight thrust right from your chin to the mitt. It went "pop" when my fist hit it.

"Timing and balance is the secret," Maloney said. "And breathing. Let your punch lead you in, snort and push out on your stomach muscles as the blow lands. Proper breathing amplifies the power of the punch."

The mitt went "pow" when my fist hit it.

Pretty good, I thought. I did what he said to do, but understanding what he said and doing it isn't the same. Jim wasn't pleased with my performance. When he explained my mistakes, it made all the difference in the world. The mitt went "WHOMP" under the smashing blow.

"But I find it easier to do it this way," one student complained.

"What's easy and what's effective are two different things," Maloney responded with his ever-present smile.

He showed two other punches. The "Overhand" is like the swing of a sledgehammer and, when you do it right, it hits just about as hard. Another — he calls it the "Slider" — is useful if you're crouched down low, under the attacker's knife thrust. Palm up, the punch comes up from under his guard and drives right through his solar plexus.

16.3 Using Your Knife

With the expert training going on in prison exercise yards nowadays, you need to understand knife-fighting techniques. And with the techniques Maloney teaches, you can defend yourself with the three-inch blade you carry in your pocket, or the rescue knife most cops carry.

There are probably as many different techniques as there are instructors teaching them. But Maloney's were developed from experience. Standing in front of the class with his traditional neck and wrist beads, he asked if we knew why Indians wear such decorations. "Where are knife attacks often directed? Neck and wrists."

He favors holding the knife in the strong hand, blade to the rear with the back against your forearm. This is the least intimidating to viewers and most protective of the knife. You could even use the knife as you would a baton or flashlight in a forearm block.

If you are trained in the martial arts, there are many things you can do to defend yourself, some more practical than others. But Maloney knows most of us aren't going to become Black Belts. From all his martial disciplines, he concentrates on a half-dozen principles that are easy to remember, and quickly become natural reactions to an attack.

Suppose you are armed only with your rescue or hunting knife. Maloney's techniques turn you into a formidable opponent that a mugger will quickly wish he'd never challenged — if he lives long enough to have a wish.

If someone swings a blade at you, roll in the same direction as the attack, so you move away and duck under the threat. Then you can bring your knife hand toward your chest, thumb side toward you, and thrust it straight out and

Think only a "sissy" would hold a knife this way? Try it. A knife or ball point pen can be thrust with lethal force with a push from the protected palm.

up into the attacker. That's the "Front Strike." Or, with the knife held as described, you could do a straight-forward punch with a flip of the wrist to drive the cutting edge of the blade into the attacker. Maloney calls that the "Outside Slash." If you're in poor position with the blade to the right, turning your palm up (like the slider punch) puts it to the left and you do an "Inside Slash."

Scumbag's partner comes up behind you. As you recover from the front strike, the knife is in perfect position for a strike to the rear.

If the attacker is wearing a heavy leather jacket, put your weak hand on your strong wrist to add power to the outside slash as you step forward and left (for right-handers). Then do a figure-8. Turn your hand over and slash inside, as you step on the right. Cup your weak hand over your strong hand and the forward strike has even *more* power.

Notice the similarity between the bare hand punches and the knife grip moves Maloney teaches. He's an advocate of the KISS principle — keep it simple, stupid.

Describing Maloney's techniques in much greater detail would do you a disservice. It might lead you to believe you could learn to do it all merely by reading this. It was obvious to me that, even in the class he taught, students did not learn from his explanation. They did learn, however, when they tried the moves as Maloney pointed out to each one what they weren't doing right. Then they could see and appreciate the difference.

16.4 Keep Low

When an attacker comes at you, he's looking straight ahead. When you roll with his thrust and stay low, you're out of his primary vision. He doesn't pick up on your counterattack as quickly as he would if you were standing straight up. But everyone wanted to straighten up before they punched. Marquis of Queensberry rules, perhaps?

Maloney bisected the room with a rope tied about chest high. The defender on one side of the rope had to make his moves against the attacker on the other side. And he had to do it *under* the rope. The rope twanged many times before the idea got across.

16.5 Best Defense Is Good Offense

"The key to defense against the knife is ATTACK," Maloney explained. "If someone has swung a knife at you, he's committed. You've got no choice but to take him out as quickly as you can before he swings again."

Your counterattack may be just parrying his thrust, as you turn into a shooting stance while drawing your gun. It may be your choice, or necessity, to turn out his lights with a straight punch to the jaw. Perhaps your best shot is to deflate his ego with a slider-jab to the diaphragm. If he caught you with nothing more than your rescue knife for defense, you may have no choice but to use it to end the confrontation quickly.

Fights like this don't last long. Of his more than 100 championship bouts, Maloney says only a few lasted longer than ten seconds. On the street, the last thing you want is for the attacker to strike again. If you're built like me, you can't afford a wrestling match. He might win. And you can bet he never heard of the Marquis of Queensberry. You've got to be able to end the assault with a couple of quick, powerful punches.

16.6 Special Concerns

Ayoob adds a few considerations for police officers:

"If you're threatened with a knife, the power of the gun is its ability to deter, to defuse the situation," he said. "If you draw a nightstick, it's a challenge, a slap in the face. It's like telling him you can defeat him with a lesser weapon. If you draw your gun, an obviously more potent weapon, you give the guy a face-saving way out of the situation. None of his buddies would blame him for backing down from the gun."

And there's another consideration for anyone who uses a gun in the face of a knife threat. Perhaps potential witnesses aren't looking your way, but there could well be people within earshot. To the traditional "DON'T MOVE!" add three more words, "DROP THAT WEAPON!" It can help to establish the fact that the aggressor is armed.

All this will help you in court, or at least through the police investigation. And that's really an optimistic outlook. With the defensive skills you learn after reading this book, you're more likely to be the one who survives the encounter. And I'd trade getting killed for a court appearance – any day.

17

"Humane" Devices

Society has long looked for something that will help police restrain a subject without causing harmful effects. Some are rather colorful and some somewhat less than "humane." Tear gas was developed back in World War I. The rubber bullets used in Northern Ireland today are an attempt to be "humane" in riot control.

This search has produced a variety of devices designed for a policeman's personal use; one could spend the rest of this book extolling or berating them. The simple fact is that a panacea has yet to be found.

Speaking more generally on force, Andy Casavant of the Midwest Tactical Training Institute says, "There is no magical cure-all for our use of force options. Officers and administrators are constantly looking for that one single item that can do it all. Believe me, it just doesn't exist and probably never will."

For the officer well-trained in defensive tactics, most nonlethal devices are "crutches" he shouldn't need. But they could be a help to the officer who is less confident of his own physical skills. Some are designed to work against multiple adversaries. For those reasons, they are mentioned here.

17.1 Mechanical Devices

The subject is an unarmed, but violent, mental patient. He really doesn't know what he's doing. You don't want to kill him, but you must get him under control. Net the poor fish. *Captur-Net* takes a lesson from the purse fisherman. Two officers can fling the net to entangle such a subject and get him under control.

The *Power Staf* is a kinetic device that works with compressed air — a pneumatic piston impact weapon. It can deliver multiple body blows against an attacker up to seven feet away, with the nonlethal effectiveness of baton blows.

The stun grenade will get someone's attention with a loud bang and bright flash, but no harmful shrapnel. It serves its purpose in tactical situations, but you're not likely to have one in your pocket.

17.2 Electronic Devices

Stun guns have been in the news in recent years, usually in an unfavorable light. But the public's aversion to these devices is understandable when you recognize the history of electric devices.

The electric chair is hardly a nonlethal compliance device, but people think of it when you mention electricity. Writer Tony Lesce tells of other applications that cast a bad light:

During World War II, the 'telephone' was used by the Gestapo to aid interrogations. A military field telephone has a hand-cranked magneto to provide ringing power. When interrogators applied electrodes to sensitive parts of the body and turned the crank, intense pain was induced. During the Algerian War, the French used an adaptation of the telephone technique taught at the "St. Joan of Arc Interrogation School" run by French intelligence agents. During the disorders of the 1960s, some officers used cattle prods against the demonstrators.

In psychiatry today, electroshock therapy has fallen into disfavor after a few fatalities showed it was not as safe a treatment as first thought. Then you have the mad scientist movies, with Tesla coils and spark gaps lighting the laboratory where Dr. Frankenstein's monster was made. All this reinforces the negative image of electricity.

Then came electronic devices designed for police.

The *Source*, no longer made, was a flashlight on one end and short electrodes on the other. When pressed against an aggressive subject and turned on, the pain-producing shock caused a retractive reflex. The *Nova XR5000* is designed to incapacitate a combative subject by inducing muscle spasms. It produces a high-voltage current that causes loss of muscular control, leaving the subject dazed but conscious.

Tony Lesce tested these devices. He found them nonlethal and confirmed that they basically work as claimed. But he raised more questions than he answered. Electricity can be unpredictable when wet. Sparking can ignite combustible vapors. And it's too easy to misuse or abuse it. United Press International reported that on April 22, 1985, two New York City police officers

The *Source*, above, was a flashlight with electrodes on the back end; below, the *Nova XR5000*.

were arraigned on charges of assault for using a stun gun illegally on a subject in custody.

These devices can be used only in close contact. There is another, the *Taser*, that can shoot electrode darts into a subject some 30 feet away, and zap him with an incapacitating jolt.

17.3 Chemical Devices

You're more likely to come into contact with chemical agents, so you should be familiar with them. All chemical agent devices are color coded, to tell you what's inside. Red means CN, blue is CS, yellow is HC or smoke, green is DM, and grey means practice items. Violet is CR, a new chemical agent not used in the United States. You probably will never use DM, which is a sickening agent used by the military.

Those in a liquid carrier in an aerosol canister are either CN (red) or CS (blue). Yellow in this case means no chemical agent, just carrier medium for practice spraying.

We list them so you'll know what all the colors mean.

During World War I, the U.S. Army spent a lot of time developing a inoffensive chemical agent suitable for training the troops with gas masks.

Come to think of it, when I went through boot camp in World War II, we had to go through the gas house. It was enough to make a grown man cry.

While we use the term "gas," tear gas is really a solid, a fine powder "dust" that is carried by something else: smoke in a grenade, or liquid in an aerosol container.

The substance developed was *Chloraceteophenone*; just remember it as CN. That's tear gas, a lacrimating agent, color-coded red. When a person is exposed to it, his tear ducts flow, his eyes smart and his eyelids try to close. A burning sensation is felt on moist skin. Get away from the gas and the effects soon dissipate. Flushing with water helps. There are no adverse aftereffects and it's relatively easy to clean up an area after exposure.

In 1960, the U.S. Army adopted a new chemical agent called *Orthochlor-benzalmalonontrile*. Remember it as CS, color-coded blue. This is an agent more potent than CN, an irritant that's more effective than CN against a large mob. The effects of CS include extreme burning sensation of the eyes, flowing tears, involuntary closing of the eyes, coughing and chest tightening, sinus and nasal drip, extreme burning sensation on areas of moist skin, such as the face, armpits, and groin. If you use it indoors, it's more difficult to clean up than CN.

But a different characteristic becomes important when you put these substances in an aerosol container.

17.3.1 Aerosol Sprays

When the big controversy over "mace" made national network news a few years ago, I witnessed some and read many reports of tests by law enforcement agencies evaluating a variety of aerosol devices. They all reached similar conclusions.

CN vaporizes much more readily than CS. Yes, the milder of the two produces a quicker reaction when "sprayed" in a stream into an aggressor's face. From among the various manufacturers, you can get either CN or CS in an aerosol device.

A simple test proved it to me. Put a piece of cellophane tape under each eye, so you don't feel the burning sensation. Then smear a drop of CS spray on one. It takes some 20 seconds or so before the vapors hit your eye. Try it with CN under the other eye and it closes in a second or three.

Obviously, the better choice for an aerosol spray is CN, and it's the least likely to bring undesirable consequences down on your head.

17.3.2 First Aid

It's probably your department policy that if you gas someone, you have to provide first aid. Fortunately, some common sense practices apply to both CN and CS.

Remove the subject to a clear area and face him into the wind. Don't let him rub or scratch. This only pushes the particulates deeper into the skin. This is usually enough if exposure isn't severe. Flushing the eyes with cool, clear water will speed recovery, but tell him to use ten times as much water as he feels necessary. Always remove contact lenses before flushing the eyes.

If his clothes have become contaminated, take them off. But be careful; you can pick up the agent on your hands and contaminate yourself. Normal cleaning will restore his clothing. Obviously, don't use any creams, salves, or dressings on irritated skin. That just traps the agent and prolongs its effects.

Exposure to chemical agents makes it seem as if you can't get your breath. That's a psychological effect on normal people. But if someone is showing signs of severe or prolonged effects, difficulty breathing, severe chest pain, or contamination of wounds, get medical help.

18

Legal Concerns

It's unfortunate, but we are in a vulnerable profession. We are *required* to use whatever force is necessary to protect citizens, yet other citizens are quick to challenge our use of any force.

Your best defense against such a suit is showing that you are well trained in all the tools of your trade, describing how you acted in good faith, and explaining that you used *only* the lowest degree of force permitted by the actions of the subject. Notice that two out of three defenses concern your communicating clearly to the court.

18.1 Civil Rights Act of 1971

You hear lawyers refer to 1983. They don't mean a year. They mean Section 1983 of the Civil Rights Act of 1971, which says:

> Every person who, under color of any statute, ordinance, regulation, custom, or usage, of any state or territory, subjects, or causes to be subjected, any citizen of the United States or other person within the jurisdiction thereof of the deprivation of any rights, privileges or immunities secured by the constitution and laws, shall be liable to the party injured in an action at law, suit in equity, or other proper proceeding for redress.

18.2 You WILL Be Sued

It really doesn't matter that you were fully justified in using force to accomplish your purpose as a police officer. Anyone can sue but, thank goodness, not everyone wins.

Just imagine you're passing a store front. You see through the show window a suspicious character holding a gun on the clerk at the cash register. He sees you. Before you can do little more than dive for cover, the subject bursts out of the door shooting. You return fire. You hit the subject in the body several times, but he keeps on shooting. You take a hit. Finally, a well-aimed shot into the offender's head ends the battle. He dies. You survive.

This actually happened in Illinois. That bullet is still in the officer, because it would be too dangerous to operate and remove it.

Obviously, a justified shoot. Right? Certainly. But that doesn't stop law suits. The offender's family sued the officer for using excessive force. They lost their case, but the officer had to spend money out of his pocket for his legal defense.

18.3 YOU Can Sue

There have been many examples of police countersuits, but one as recent as December 1986 makes a powerful point: a cop won damages from a woman, according to our local newspaper.

A Norwich, Connecticut, policeman, who was sued for police brutality, was awarded $500 by a federal judge. Officer Kevin McKeon and his partner Andrew Bartha were sued by a woman who claimed she was deprived of her civil rights when the officers broke her arm while subduing her.

McKeon filed a counterclaim saying he was the victim because the woman bit him and struck him several times during the incident. After a two-day trial in November, U.S. District Judge Jose A. Cabranes ruled *in favor* of the police officer.

"The judge took the opportunity to send a message to all law enforcement officers in Connecticut that they are no longer sitting ducks in civil rights actions," said McKeon's attorney Joseph Morelli of Hartford.

18.4 Writing Reports

Writing a complete report on an incident where you had to use force, any amount of force, is much more important to you than satisfying your sergeant.

Stop to consider that, in most jurisdictions, the discovery process gives an opposing attorney a copy of every departmental report filed concerning a case. You — whether you testify as a prosecution witness, civil defendant, or criminal defendant — will be cross-examined on the basis of the report you wrote perhaps two years ago.

"When compared with your sworn testimony, what your report does NOT contain may be more crucial than what it does," says Atty. Walter MacDonald. "You will almost certainly be asked, 'Now officer, is your memory of these events better today than it was back when you wrote your report?' Facts and details stated from the witness stand, but omitted from the report, will be branded 'recent contrivances.' The argument will be made that if the incident had happened as you now say it did, your report would have coincided with your version of the facts."

A practicing attorney, MacDonald is Training Officer and Tactical Team Leader for the Plymouth County (Massachusetts) Sheriff's Department, so he knows whereof he speaks — from both sides of the bench. He has seen good and bad examples of justifying the use of force where it counts, in court.

Whenever you use any amount of force, your report must clearly and completely state the facts justifying the kind and amount of force you used. If any lesser means of control were tried and failed, put that in your report, too.

Too many department policies simply state "the officer shall file a full and complete report." This leaves it up to you to decide what to include. Unless you get positive identification of witnesses and other facts immediately at the scene, that information is often lost forever.

When you use force, you feel stress. The more force you must exert to subdue a subject, the more stress you feel — and the more likely you are to skimp on the report. In this sort of situation, it's in your best interest to take whatever time you need to develop that report.

Department policies should include a specific and detailed section on reporting. MacDonald suggests the following information should always be included:

1. An account of events leading up to the use of force.
2. A precise description of the incident and reasons for employing force.
3. A description of the type of force used (including weapon, if any) and the manner in which it was used.
4. A description of the injuries suffered, if any, and the treatment given, if known; along with photographs, if any.
5. A list of all participants and witnesses to the incident.

Although reports are written for internal departmental use, they can go further. A report explaining the use of force should be carefully composed, leaving no opening for misinterpretation, nor reflecting unfavorably on the officer when it is read by a judge and jury who weren't there when it happened — and have never experienced the threat you faced.

18.5 Liability Defense

You might be sued for something you did, like the officer who shot the armed robber who was shooting at him. That was a good shooting and the officer won the case. But you could be sued because you made a mistake that put you in position of having to use force you might otherwise not have needed to use.

Suppose you sneak up on a bad guy, then step out into the open to challenge him. He sees you are vulnerable and pulls a gun. You shoot in self-defense and would probably be found justified by a firearms review board. But a lawyer suing you will say you caused the suspect to draw his gun by exposing yourself. If you had remained behind cover, you would not have needed deadly force. That's his job.

There is always the question whether some lesser degree of force might have accomplished your purpose, without resorting to "excessive" force. That's why you need to have an explanation ready that lesser force was tried and failed—or was inappropriate—and why. Being able to give reasons for your actions will help a reasonable jury to understand.

There are two types of damages assessed in a lawsuit. Compensatory damages "compensate" the plaintiff for his suffering. Punitive damages are assessed when those 12 reasonable men and women of the jury are so incensed at some outrageous act, they want to "punish" the defendant. Punitive damages can be assessed against an individual officer. And it doesn't have to be a big deal.

Dr. Parsons does a lot of expert analysis and case consultation defending policemen and agencies against such suits. He had one case where an officer had shot and killed a suspect. The lawyer asked him what firearms training he'd had.

"Well, not much since the academy," the officer replied. "Mostly movies."

"What did the trainees do during these movies?" the lawyer asked.

"Well, most of the guys slept," he responded truthfully. "Some guys made paper airplanes and flew them around."

Parsons explained that the jury was so outraged at the officer's attitude, they awarded punitive damages. Flying paper airplanes is not a reasonable activity for professional police officers in firearms training, and the jury will decide on the basis of reasonableness.

An 18-year-old kid threw a soda can out the car window. A policeman saw the littering infraction and tried to pull the car over. The kid tromped on the gas and a high-speed chase ensued. The car was finally cornered and stopped. By this time, a half dozen officers surrounded the vehicle. One officer held a shotgun to the kid's shoulder as he tried to handcuff him. The gun went off unintentionally and blew the kid's shoulder off.

Obviously, there are a number of charges you could bring against the kid. But the suit painted a pitiful picture of an all-American boy maimed for life because of a littering complaint. Is that a reasonable consequence for such a petty crime?

"You have to be able to explain why you acted as you did, why the suspect's actions left you no alternative but to exert the level of force you used," Parsons explains.

In reports, avoid police-ese phrases. "I subdued the subject with reasonable force," doesn't tell the jury anything. If you hit him in the leg, say you hit him in the leg — because he had just punched you in the mouth, and you knew that by hitting the pressure point at the side of his knee, you would put him down so you could handcuff him. You have to paint a word picture that a jury can understand and consider reasonable for the reasons you explain — should that report be brought into court.

Never get so excited that you shout obscenities as you "exit your vehicle to apprehend the perpetrator." Your testimony must be verbatim, and you must consider how street language sounds to the housewife or school teacher on the jury.

"Our response to that is 'SIR'," Parsons adds. "Our definition of 'sir' is someone who has no redeeming social value. Use phrases like 'Sir, you'll have to come with me.' Calmly tell him, 'Sir, don't hurt yourself,' as you apply a pain compliance technique."

When you are sued, Parsons offers this advice:

1. Don't panic. Most excessive force suits aren't won.

2. Don't sit on your report. Get evidence together immediately.

3. Keep records of *everything* related to the case: copies of department policies, copies of reports, witness statements, your academy scores. And keep copies for your files.

4. Keep those files in your possession. When someone needs a copy, make one for him, and keep your files complete.

5. Don't think a seemingly frivolous suit isn't serious. Lawyers who handle such cases get perhaps a third of the judgment. On a $100,000 suit, that's some $33,000 and a lawyer will work pretty hard to earn that amount of money for a week's work.

6. It's to your advantage to help the lawyer representing you do a good job.

7. In a bifurcated trial, where you and your city are being sued separately, you should have your own attorney. The lawyer representing your employer may find it to his client's advantage to put you in a bad light.

8. Go over the case with your lawyer, identify any areas where you might be criticized, and start preparing defenses for those points, should they come up.

18.6 Importance of Certification

Certification represents training to a level of acceptable competency. It is critical in high-liability areas of driving a car, baton, handcuffing, defensive tactics, CPR. A certificate gives you ready evidence that you were properly trained by a qualified instructor. *It doesn't protect you from lawsuits*; medical doctors and Ph.D. experts are challenged all the time. But it can help.

Successful completion of department training should be entered into your record. It must not only show that you were there, but what was taught and what was your performance achievement.

Outside training consultants should provide your agency with documentation on their program, a syllabus outlining the lesson plan.

Some policemen like to paper their wall with certificates. But all the certificates in the world aren't going to help you if, after getting all that training, you go out and do the same dumb things you did before.

19

The Deadly Decision

If you become expert in the defensive tactics we've discussed, you have many alternative options. You may well cool a situation before it reaches the point of deadly force. But escalation can be instantaneous. Then you have no choice.

Just when can you use that gun?

That's a question that plagues police officers, and its answer is sometimes vague. It depends upon a lot of things.

First, recognize that our society holds the value of human life highly. Any time a life is taken, extra effort is exerted to determine the facts and decide the justification. Whenever you shoot, you can count on a thorough investigation, and likely a long time will be spent in court. The investigating IAD officer may feel like patting your back as he pins on a medal, but you *will* be put through the wringer.

19.1 Old Wives' Tales

Now, let's get rid of some well known machismos you may have heard.

"If I know he has committed a felony and he tries to flee, I can shoot him."
The U.S. Supreme Court, in the Garner vs. Tennessee decision, held that shooting a youthful burglar trying to flee with his loot was an unreasonable seizure of his person. The "Fleeing Felon" laws of some 19 states were wiped out with one stroke of the judicial pen. But police departments' policies had

long since precluded the fleeing felon rule. Technically, the juvenile fleeing from the stolen car he just wrecked is a felon. Would you shoot him? Of course not. The court really didn't do anything that police policy hadn't already done.

With widespread news media coverage of this decision, however, the popular warning, "Stop or I'll shoot," used in old police movies, has no meaning anymore.

"If you shoot someone, then discover he's unarmed, drop an untraceable gun on him." Just how untraceable do you think a gun is? Was it an heirloom you inherited, an old gun you found in the attic of an old house you bought? Okay, so you bought a "Saturday Night Special" just for this purpose. Do you think you're the only one who knows you've got that gun? If you use a "drop" gun, you demonstrate malice, forethought, and intentional altering of evidence. Those are elements of premeditated murder. Try explaining that in court.

Besides, three out of four police involved shootings do *not* result in death. Your wounded suspect becomes the "victim," who will testify to everything that makes you look bad.

Be assured right up front, truth is the strongest weapon you have. Accordingly, there are certain truths that you must know.

19.2 Basic Truths

No court will look favorably on your pulling the trigger if you could have avoided it.

This principle was debated in the news media in relation to the Bernhard Goetz case. Goetz, as you may recall, used a gun against three muggers in a New York subway. A national newsweekly stated, "To justify violent self-defense, a person must prove his life is in danger."

A retired district court judge took exception. "To justify violent self-defense, a person must *reasonably believe* that his life is in danger. The reasonableness is tested under the circumstance in which the person finds himself at the time. . . . It is not a course of action that a person may take when not in exigent circumstances, and after time for cool reflection. When confronted with a crisis, a human being acts in accordance with the situation as he perceived it at that time."

It boils down to one basic truth: *You are justified in using deadly force only to stop a felonious assault that you reasonably believe threatens death or grievous bodily harm to you or someone else.*

This is extended somewhat for police officers. If the subject is fleeing for the purpose of immediately killing another person, the court will take that into consideration. Most deadly force policies include a proviso for imminent danger.

Don't depend on that old "life and property" phrase either. Even if your state law says "protection of life and property," the court will view your case on the basis of the "judgment of the reasonable man." Is it reasonable to shoot the neighborhood kid making off with a stereo?

As the retired judge points out, there's another hitch. Since you can shoot only to stop a grievous threat, what happens when the felon tries to run?

19.3 When Threat Ends

The suspect threatened you, so you properly pulled your gun. He sees it and decides greener pastures lie elsewhere. He runs. If you pursue him and holler, "Stop or I'll shoot!"—who is the aggressor? Who is causing the new confrontation? If, at that point, he turns and shoots you, might not he claim self-defense?

The fact that you may have been justified in shooting to stop his threat does not carry over after the threat has ended. The court might well view your motive then as a malicious or misguided intent to perform an illegal punishment against the transgressor.

19.4 When Threat Begins

Neither are you justified in using deadly force a moment before an attack begins.

You'd be surprised how many cops have asked, "Do I have to wait for him to fire the first shot?" Obviously not. If you can articulate your reasons to *believe* that a grievous threat is about to begin, you can employ the "preemptive first strike." But just *when* is a grievous threat about to begin?

The subject's threat to come back and kill you tomorrow is certainly not a threat of imminent danger to you. It may be an empty threat, just his way of looking macho. The threat must be imminent and unavoidable.

An example I use in training policemen explains the elements of a deadly threat.

You're walking down a sidewalk. A man comes out of a sporting goods store up the block with a new baseball bat. The bat gives him the *capability* of doing deadly harm. He turns your way and approaches to within three feet. His proximity now gives him the *opportunity*. But you wouldn't shoot, would you? Then he raises the bat and starts to swing at your head. Now you are in *jeopardy*, and should be justified in defending yourself.

The three elements of the shooting requirement are (1) capability, (2) opportunity, and (3) jeopardy. Unless all three are present, there is *no* justification for deadly force.

19.5 Decision Not Yours

You notice, I don't use the term "shooting decision." You don't decide to shoot. You react to the circumstances confronting you. The assailant puts you in a position where you have no choice but to shoot. So I say the "shooting decision" is really made by the aggressor, who presents you with those three elements.

Do you "shoot to kill?" If your case goes to a court hearing, you can bet you'll be asked if you intended to kill the perpetrator. Your answer should be obvious, if you've articulated your reasons for believing his actions threatened you or another with imminent and unavoidable grievous bodily harm or death.

NO. You did NOT shoot to kill.

You shot only to stop his felonious assault against you or another person. It doesn't matter that you're a pistol champion and could place your shot where it would only wound him. Wounding or killing is irrelevant and immaterial.

You shot only to stop his felonious assault.

19.6 A Capsule Review

Just what is "deadly force?" A gun? Not necessarily. One of the best definitions I've seen is in a model deadly force policy for police: ". . . is that force, by whatever means imposed, which is likely to cause death or grave injury, or which creates some specified degree of risk that a reasonable and prudent person would consider likely to cause death or grave injury."

Deadly force is *any* force that results in or threatens death. The implement might be a gun, knife, length of rope (if it's around your neck), or a baseball bat.

The threat doesn't start until the aggressor lunges. If he were to stumble and fall, the threat ends. Your window of justification exists while the attack is actually in progress. It is then that you are in "exigent circumstances," as the judge said.

It is during this window that you can articulate your reasons to believe that you or someone else is threatened with death or grievous bodily harm. And that's when you can know you are justified in making the "shooting decision."

20

Training Issues Involving Women

If you ask Elizabeth Callahan, National Women's Police Pistol Champion and a firearms instructor for the Metropolitan Police Department in Washington, D.C., she'll say female officers are nothing special. Her point is that they must deal with the same situations on the street as the males.

Yes, women lack upper body strength, but so do many males. I never was much good on the chinning bar, either.

There are considerations peculiar to women because of their different structure that should not be overlooked — hand size and strength, and arm length which can be a problem when training with shoulder weapons.

Cathy Lane, a former police officer and now co-director with her husband Jerry of the OffShoots Training Institute, agrees. But females are traditionally different than males because of their social upbringing.

What these two gals have taught me in training is significant.

20.1 Different Backgrounds

Lane told me that males are generally handled more as babies and become involved in games of strategy and team competition that includes tussling and punching. Females are talked to more as babies and do more things alone, such as arts and crafts. They must be taught how to both deliver and receive a punch, because it's a totally new experience for most of them. Most women

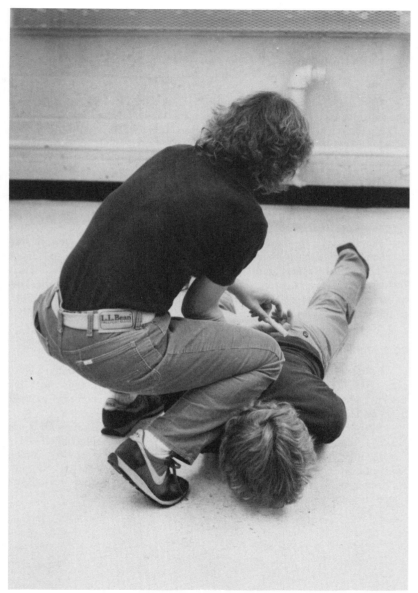

Two females in our *Kubotan* class paired up with each other to practice defensive tactics. They are Nan Frantz of the New York State Department of Correctional Services, and Helen Gray of the Scituate, Massachusetts, Police Department.

can't go toe-to-toe in a slugout with a man. But they can do tough physical tasks if they are properly trained to use their body, especially hips and legs, correctly.

Because females didn't fight as kids, they need to "feel" the punch. If the instructor is a chivalrous male and holds back, his female students aren't really prepared for the street.

"Females need lots of good hands-on training," Lane says. "And it's not a good idea to pair up women with each other exclusively in defensive tactics classes. They won't be dealing with just women on the street."

This is not to say that many men don't need the same kind of training. I thought I could punch — until that course at the Lethal Force Institute, where instructor Jim Maloney addressed the subject of punching. My punch lacked force, because I had never learned how to really throw a punch in ernest.

So, while this chapter addresses women, it is just as appropriate to many men. See, I'm really not chauvinistic. I once wanted to buy a tie that said "MCP" (Male Chauvinist Pig) — but my wife wouldn't let me.

Females come from different backgrounds than males. They grew up with different values. Regardless of what you think of women in police work, some have accomplished much more than any man could have in certain circumstances. Sometimes, a female officer can use her excellent verbalization skills to resolve a situation where a male officer, oriented to physical solutions, couldn't. The boisterous bar patron would be embarrassed by "hitting a girl."

20.2 Training Needs

Female officers need training in verbalization skills and developing a command presence, in giving orders, in taking charge, in taking abuse, in being assertive and confident yet feminine. These are all things contrary to their heritage, but necessary to becoming a good cop.

"She should not try to be masculine," says Lane. "A woman who is not herself is often distasteful to both her fellow officers and to the public."

"Women have a strong desire to learn and are very receptive to training from a positive, informed trainer. Go into more detail, cover the basics. Trainers need to learn what natural skills females possess and develop the areas in which they are lacking," she adds.

21

A Word of Caution

Throughout your study of defensive tactics, you see references to "pain" or "pain compliance technique." Now, you know that different people have different tolerances to pain. While a pain compliance technique can be very effective, there's always the chance that it won't work.

"People who are on drugs or mentally disturbed may not respond to pain," Dr. Parsons says. "One officer told me he used a pain compliance technique and it sobered the subject right up. That could well happen but it might not. That's the problem with the short stick, chemical agents, even the baton, as well as hand-holds designed to cause pain.

"We had one case where four officers were holding an inmate down. The guy was tossing those officers around the cell like rag dolls. During the autopsy, they didn't find any PCP because there are so many variations it takes a specialized lab to detect it."

People under the influence of phencyclidine (PCP, or angel dust), first developed as an anesthetic in the 1950s but taken off the legal market, and methamphetamines, stimulants leading to hallucinations, have been known to do superhuman feats, like lifting the ends of cars. To say you're going to control such a person with pain is ludicrous. The proliferation of drugs has influenced law enforcement in this country — as has the recent popularity of knives not designed for the cook, fisherman, hunter or camper.

The old static techniques of the 1960s and early 1970s don't work any more. Nowadays, defensive tactics are much more dynamic. There is a much greater interchange of information among instructors through such organizations as the Justice System Training Association. Techniques have become more fluid, more flexible. Rather than formal rituals, these techniques are options that, when you understand the principles, may be applied in many ways.

Defensive tactics have become more science-based, developed by street-wise instructors in consultation with medical experts. As a result, defensive tactics today must meet three criteria:

1. *Techniques must work on the street.* Learning the classic martial arts in the gym can be fun. But if they don't translate to practical techniques the officer can remember and use, they don't do him much good. He'll revert to traditional scuffling and perhaps be hurt. Techniques must be usable by officers of varying age and physical condition.

2. *Techniques must be court-defensible.* Techniques that can be shown to have a high propensity for control with a low propensity for doing damage are more easily justified in court.

3. *Programs must be administratively feasible.* Most department instructors can't get 75 hours for DT training, because most training budgets aren't that big. So they must design programs they can sell to their administrative heads. It might be as little as a repetitive ten-minute exercise with the baton at roll call, as one large agency does. Some of its officers have become more proficient with the baton than the instructor, because of repetitive practice.

All the tools and techniques a policeman uses must be evaluated on this potential for control vs. damage. The baton can be misused. Suits involving flashlights have resulted from misuse, not from using them with proper baton techniques. Even the simple finger flex (grabbing a finger and bending it backwards), while there's no question it causes pain, crank a little too hard and you've broken the finger. Anchoring the elbow and bending the hand down with pressure on the knuckles can be shown to provide control with much less likelihood of causing damage.

There are a lot of "nice-to-know" techniques. It looks great in Bruce Lee movies to watch him take the knife away from a snarling assailant. But the officer, who doesn't have the opportunity to practice every day, isn't likely to be so proficient he can do it without getting cut. Good techniques are those you can learn, practice realistically, and perform well enough that you gain confidence in your ability to use them.

In your study of defensive tactics, you'll pick up a few principles from each of the different disciplines. No one expects you to become a "black belt" in everything. But you can become expert enough in the practical application of those tactics that suit your purpose, so you will be able to handle an uncooperative or even aggressive subject at a lower rung on the ladder of force continuum. That can save you a lot of time and inconvenience going to court to justify your smashing the guy's face, or blowing him away.

22

Consultants

Capt. George J. Armbruster
Lafayette Parish Sheriff's Dept.
316 W. Main Street
Lafayette, LA 70501
(318) 232-9211

Massad F. Ayoob
Lethal Force Institute
P.O. Box 122
Concord, NH 03301
(603) 224-6814

Andy Casavant
Midwest Tactical Training Institute
2070 Audubon Drive
Glendale Heights, IL 60139
(312) 529-5548

Jim Maloney
Special Tactical and Response
P.O. Box 504
Lower Sackville, NS B4C 3G4
(902) 861-1068

Roland Ouellette
Conn. Law Enforcement Training
    Institute
P.O. Box 697
Avon, CT 06001
(203) 677-5936

Kevin Parsons, Ph.D.
Justice System Training Assn.
Box 356
Appleton, WI 54912
(414) 731-8893

John Desmedt
U.S. Secret Service
Washington, DC 22032

Sgt. Gary T. Klugiewicz
Milwaukee County Sheriff's Dept.
821 W. State St.
Milwaukee, WI 53233
(414) 278-4700

Jerry D. Lane
OffShoots Training Institute
P.O. Box 550334
Atlanta, GA 30355-2834
(404) 365-8998

James Lindell
National Law Enforcement
  Training Center
3238 Gillham Road
Kansas City, MO 64109
(816) 444-7697

Robert K. Lindsey
572 Randolph Avenue
Harahan, LA 70123
(504) 738-5258

Deputy Walter J. MacDonald
Plymouth County Sheriff's Dept.
26 Cottage St.
Brockton, MA 02401
(617) 580-2110

John G. Peters
Defensive Tactics Institute
P.O. Box 14872, Station G, NE
Albuquerque, NM 87111
(505) 243-7985

Tim Powers
Fitness Institute for Police, Fire
  and Rescue
816 6th Street
Menasha, WI 54952
(414) 725-2368

Bruce K. Siddle
PPCT Management Systems
P.O. Box 175
Waterloo, IL 62298
(618) 939-7575

Joseph Truncale, Ph.D.
Professional Police & Security
  Systems
P.O. Box 261
Glenview, IL 60025
(312) 729-7671

Daniel Vega
Catalyst
4016 N. Wilson Drive
Shorewood, WI 53211
(414) 332-7073